The INFLUENCE of BEAUMONT and FLETCHER ON RESTORATION DRAMA

BY

JOHN HAROLD WILSON, Ph.D.

HASKELL HOUSE PUBLISHERS Ltd.

Publishers of Scarce Scholarly Books

NEW YORK. N. Y. 10012

1969

First Published 1928

HASKELL HOUSE PUBLISHERS Ltd.
Publishers of Scarce Scholarly Books
280 LAFAYETTE STREET
NEW YORK, N. Y. 10012

Library of Congress Catalog Card Number: 68–57458

Standard Book Number 8383–0645–4

Printed in the United States of America

INTRODUCTION

THE PURPOSE of this dissertation is to examine into the possible influence of the Beaumont and Fletcher dramas on the comedies of the Restoration. Generally the Restoration is considered that period beginning with the return of Charles II and the re-opening of the theatres in 1660, and ending arbitrarily in 1700. However, since the works of certain dramatists who continued on beyond the last date—notably Farquhar and Vanbrugh—were in the tradition of the Restoration drama, they also have been considered.

Since it is always difficult to prove a positive influence, the writer has sought to evade the error of dogmatism. He has shown first that the writers of the Restoration were well acquainted with the works of Beaumont and Fletcher, on the stage and in print; that the Restoration audiences had a distinct taste for their plays; second, that critics and dramatists united in praise of the two Jacobeans for their work; third, that Restoration writers altered and borrowed from the Beaumont and Fletcher plays; and finally that the work of the Restoration writers in many important phases is like their models.

The sea of influences which inundated the writers of the Restoration is still poorly charted. Numerous studies have appeared on the French influence, long regarded as the most important of all. Little or nothing has been done on Spanish or Italian influence; yet Spanish novels, in translation, were widely read; Spanish plays were often translated, and troupes of Italian actors, in Italian dramatic entertainments, were popular in London toward the close of the century. Yet of all influences, that of the precedent English drama seems to the writer most important.

The dramatists of the Restoration should be considered not so much literary men as men of the theatre, that is, as craftsmen. To speak of influences working on the man of genius, is often to discuss vague and unprovable intangibles. But the dramatists of the Restoration were rarely geniuses; the rank and file, who carried on the tradition of sophisticated comedy, were hack-writers, borrowers—rarely has conscious plagiarism been more rampant than in this period. Like the dramatists of today, who, seeing a successful invention on the contemporary stage, immediately adapt it to their own uses, the Restoration writers followed each other slavishly, rarely inventing, rarely improving. It is a fact amazing to contemplate that for forty years or more, the important dramatic fare of the small London audiences was a type of comedy which made use of stock characters, in stock situations, utilizing stock ideas.

But there are no isolated phenomena in the history of the drama. A novelist may suddenly develop a new type of narrative, a poet may produce an important change in poetry—he has only his printer to coerce and he is sure of some kind of an audience, however small. But the dramatist is dealing with a slow and conservative institution. The audiences are accustomed to a certain type of play; the actors have become used to such and such mannerisms; the managers have seen the new fail and the old succeed, and failure is costly. The result is a tendency to keep dramatic production to the tried and safe, and to discourage innovation of any kind. We have only to look, for examples, at the condition of the modern stage—the failure of experimental theatres, the success of other theatres producing stock types of plays, made according to safe old formulae.

It is only natural that we should find the people of the Restoration, audiences, actors, managers and dramatists, looking backward to the successful plays of the immediate past. And of all the older plays, those of Beaumont and Fletcher loomed largest on the dramatic horizon.

CHAPTER I

POPULAR AND CRITICAL PRAISE

Revivals

THE POSSIBLE SOURCES of influence upon Restoration comedy may be divided into two groups: foreign (French, Spanish and Italian) and English. It is with the latter that we are concerned. The belief, prevalent for so long a time, that Restoration comedy was merely a reflection of contemporary French tastes, is now generally denied;[1] yet, while the opinion of today holds that the English comedy of the years 1660 to 1700 was based to a large extent upon the work of Elizabethan and Jacobean dramatists, the proper apportionment of such influences has been an open question.

The Restoration, at least in the person of its chief critic, John Dryden, recognized that a great part of its dramatic method was founded upon that of its predecessors, and gave due measure of regard and praise to the older dramatists.[2] It is significant that Collier, in his attack on the stage, went to the ancients and to Beaumont and Fletcher, Shakespeare and Jonson for his authorities, using contemporary foreign drama hardly at all.[3] Rarely, in Restoration criticism, do we

[1] For discussions of French influence see Miles, D. H., *The Influence of Moliere on Restoration Comedy*, and Charlanne, L., *L'Influence Francaise en Angleterre au XVIIe Siecle*. A good summary of late findings appears in Bonamy Dobree's *Restoration Comedy*. The Spanish and Italian influences have been little explored. Much has been suggested by Allardyce Nicoll, *Restoration Drama*, p. 179 ff.

[2] Dryden, John, *Essay of Dramatic Poesy* (Mitford ed., II, p. 240). "We have borrowed nothing from them, (the French) our plots are weaved in English looms; we endeavour therein to follow the variety and greatness of characters which are derived to us from Shakespeare and Fletcher; the copiousness and well-knitting of the intrigues we have from Jonson. . ."

[3] Collier, Jeremy. *A Short View of the Immorality and Profaneness of the English Stage.* 1698.

3

find mention of any other than these three dramatists; it is they who dominated the stage at the beginning of the era, before the new school had formed; and their plays composed the greater part of the stock drama of the theaters, well up into the eighteenth century. The budding school of criticism could hardly mention one without a consideration of the others; they were considered a triumvirate of artistic excellence, and each had his particular value for the Restoration. It is necessary, then, for us to consider and sift out the possible influences of each separately. Other pre-Restoration dramatists may be generally ignored. To them we find no critical references, and their plays, with rare exceptions, were no more than stop-gaps in the theatrical emptiness of the early years.

As a preliminary to the investigation of influences it is necessary first to determine how well the dramatists of the later part of the seventeenth century were acquainted with the work of their Elizabethan and Jacobean predecessors. For there are two ways through which the Restoration writers might have received inspirations and suggestions—through the actual performances of the older plays on the later stage, and through the dissemination of printed copies. The first of these is by all odds the more important. We may expect that a dramatist seeing the plays of a predecessor frequently performed and often applauded would be inspired to write in imitation of what is obviously popular. On the other hand, to turn to his library for classic examples of that which is best (according to the critics) meant for him a large element of risk. Notoriously, critics and audiences do not always see eye to eye. However, borrowings of plots, characters or scenes, would be more likely to come from the printed texts, usually of plays not popular at the moment. The plagiarism, of course, would be less easy to detect, if the source were little known.

Because of the lack of data from the opening of the theatres in 1660 until the close of the century, it is difficult to determine accurately the relative popularity of the three great dramatists. After 1702, when Genest had Dr. Burney's playbills to refer to, records are fairly accurate. Up to that time we must depend upon such scattered references as are to be found in Pepys, Downes, Gildon, and so forth. For purposes of completeness, therefore, the period of revivals has been made to extend from 1660 to 1720, although strictly speaking the Restoration, as a literary period, was practically ended by the close of the century. But, if our account of the revivals of pre-Restoration dramas cannot pretend to completeness, it can give us a fairly thorough idea of the Restoration tastes. If we find, for example, that Beaumont and Fletcher's *Rule a Wife and Have a Wife* appeared in 1660 and 1661, twice in 1662 and again in 1663-66-82-83, twice in 1685 and once more in 1697, we may be reasonably certain, since many more performances may have taken place, that the play was popular with the Restoration audiences. When we see further that the comedy was revived annually at least once (except in 1716) and sometimes twice from 1702 through 1719, and, indeed, much later, we can be more certain that the play enjoyed unbroken popularity, with a number of revivals almost equal to that of *Hamlet*.

On the other hand, when we find *The Mad Lover* appearing in 1660, twice in 1661, once in 1669 and not at all thereafter, we must be certain that the popularity of this play waned quickly, and its possibilities for influence are correspondingly slight. Again we have the case of *The Pilgrim* for which we find no records

(except of course in the list of plays divided between
the theatres) until its alteration by Vanbrugh in 1670.
It appears again in 1700 with a masque by Dryden, and
from then on was apparently very popular in its operatic form.

We must conclude that the number of revivals noted
is not in itself sufficient evidence of the popularity of
a play. It is only when we find these revivals so dis-
tributed as to cover the entire period that we can be
assured the play was satisfactory to the Restoration.
And, of course, it must not be forgotten that the formative years of Restoration comedy, roughly 1660 to 1670,
approved of some plays which are later forgotten, and
disapproved of others which were later revived and
made popular, usually because of the new taste for
opera and melodrama.

List I (appendix) gives the names of all old plays
divided between the two theatres at the opening of the
period or later. It is important here that Beaumont
and Fletcher, Shakespeare and Jonson are represented by almost all their plays. Those left out are
The Merchant of Venice and *The Tempest,* by Shakespeare, *The Two Noble Kinsmen, Wit Without Money,
The Knight of the Burning Pestle, Monsieur Thomas,
The Night Walker,* and *The Chances* by Beaumont and
Fletcher, *The Sad Shepherd,* and *The Case is Altered,*
by Jonson. Many of these appeared later. The preponderance, in sheer numbers, of what Davenant and
Killigrew must have considered valuable plays, is heav-
ily in favor of the triumvirate, with Beaumont and
Fletcher leading.

List II records all available dates of revivals of all
pre-Restoration dramas, whether mentioned in List I
or not. It is to be noticed here that the plays of Brome
and Shirley seem to have been most popular, with

Massinger and Middleton following. Brome's *The Jovial Crew* seems to have been as popular as any of the older comedies, while a notable list of Shirley's plays must have held the boards in the first decade of the period. Speaking rather generally, we may say that Brome and Shirley represent that amalgamation which was taking place before the Restoration, between the various "humor" themes of Jonson and the intrigue-romance of Fletcher; the domestic comedies of Massinger and Middleton blending in later. It is the amalgamation which is best represented by Fletcher's *The Wild Goose Chase,* a comedy which anticipated by forty years the main trend of the Restoration. However, while the brief popularity of these minor dramatists bears out the contention that the Restoration only built on the older drama, yet, when we consider that the total is only sixty-five plays, divided among at least twenty-five writers, and with a total of only one hundred and forty-nine revivals in the whole period (1660-1720), we must admit that the major dramatists had the field of influence largely to themselves. Beaumont and Fletcher, alone, are represented by a total of three hundred and forty-two revivals of thirty-nine plays in the same period.

List III shows that Shakespeare's tragedies were popular in the Restoration. *Hamlet, Julius Caesar, Macbeth, King Lear* and *Othello* have a long record of revivals. *Romeo and Juliet, Timon, Titus Andronicus* and *Troilus and Cressida* and the histories do not seem to have fared so well. *Henry VIII,* however, must have pleased with its pageantry, and *Henry IV (Henry IV, 1)* gained some popularity through Falstaff. But the comedies in general did not appeal to the Restoration. Of *All's Well that Ends Well, As You Like It, The Comedy of Erors, Love's Labor's Lost, Much*

Ado About Nothing and *The Winter's Tale* no records of revivals are to be found. *Cymbeline, Measure for Measure, The Merchant of Venice, Midsummer Night's Dream, The Taming of the Shrew, The Tempest* and *Twelfth Night* gained temporary popularity, but most of these comedies were altered early in their Restoration career, some, notably *The Tempest*, being changed almost beyond recognition. There is plenty of critical praise for Shakespeare's tragedies, but hardly a word said in the Restoration about his comedies. The comedy of the Restoration can have had little from Shakespeare.

List IV and V, dealing with the revivals of the plays of Beaumont and Fletcher and of Ben Jonson, speak for themselves. Of the popularity of Jonson's four great comedies: *The Alchemist, Bartholomew Fair, The Silent Woman,* and *Volpone* there can be no doubt. On the other hand it is evident that Beaumont and Fletcher's *The Beggars' Bush, The Chances, The Humorous Lieutenant, Rule a Wife and Have a Wife, The Scornful Lady* were equally popular. The problem then, merely from the point of view of frequency of representation, would lie between the comedies of Jonson and those of Beaumont and Fletcher.

The striking fact about Jonson's popularity is not so much that the four great comedies were so popular, but that no others were, not even the two *Everyman* comedies. Of the comedies of Beaumont and Fletcher we find that at least twenty others, besides the five named, appeared at various times and attained varying degrees of popularity. In the early years of the Restoration, Killigrew's company, which owned most of the plays of the three great dramatists, presented sixty-eight old plays (November 5, 1660-July 23, 1662) of which twenty-seven were by Beaumont and Fletcher, three by Shakespeare and three by Jonson.[4] The statements made from time to time by Downes are pertinent. He says of the Rhodes company (1660) that "the plays acted were: *The Loyal Subject, Maid in the Mill, Wild Goose Chase, Spanish Curate, Mad Lover* (by Beaumont and Fletcher) and *Wife for a Month, Rule a Wife, Woman's Prize*" (by the same authors).[5] He then mentions five others, one of which is by Shakespeare, and none by Jonson. Again he gives a list of twenty-one old plays which were revived sometime between 1663 and 1682. It includes:[6] *Philaster, The Chances* and *The Beggar's Bush* by Beaumont and Fletcher; *Cataline, Bartholomew Fair, The Devil is an Ass, Every Man in His Humor, Every Man Out of His Humor,* and *Sejanus* by Jonson; *The Merry Wives of Windsor* and *Titus Andronicus,* by Shakespeare. In addition to these Genest adds for Beaumont and Fletcher *The Double Marriage, The Night Walker, The Knight of the Burning Pestle* and *The Coxcomb.* These revivals were of plays not already in stock, otherwise Downes would hardly have mentioned them. Of the total number Beaumont and Fletcher are represented by fifteen plays; Jonson by six.

When the companies were united in 1683 Downes says "The mixt company revived several old and modern plays that were the property of Killigrew."[7] Among these were *Rule a Wife and Have a Wife, The Scornful Lady, The Beggars' Bush, The Bloody Brother, The Humorous Lieutenant,* and *The Double Marriage,* by Beaumont and Fletcher, Shakespeare's *Othello* and Jonson's *Bartholomew Fair.* And about 1692, he says again [8] among other old and modern plays appeared

---

4 Adams, J. Q.—Dramatic Records of Sir Henry Herbert, p. 116-18.
5 Genest—I, 31.
6 Genest, I. 339.
7 Genest, I, 401.
8 Genest, II, 31.

Beaumont and Fletcher's *Wit Without Money* and Shakespeare's *The Taming of a Shrew*. If Downes may be taken as any authority, revivals of the plays of Beaumont and Fletcher must have greatly exceeded in number those of either Shakespeare or Jonson.

We have also the evidence of Langbaine in 1691 that he had seen "several times acted with applause" the following by Beaumont and Fletcher: *The Beggars' Bush, The Bloody Brother, The Chances, The Elder Brother, The Humorous Lieutenant, The Island Princess, A King and No King, The Maid's Tragedy, The Night Walker, Philaster, Rule a Wife and Have a Wife, The Scornful Lady* and *Wit Without Money.* Yet, speaking of Jonson, he mentions only *Bartholomew Fair, Cataline, Everyman in His Humor* and *Volpone.* How far this, the evidence of one play goer, may be trusted is, of course, questionable. But we must add the fact that in 1694 Sir Thomas Pope Blount could assent to and quote Dryden's statement in the *Essay of Dramatic Poetry* that "their (Beaumont and Fletcher's) plays are now the most frequent and pleasant entertainments of the stage; two of theirs being acted through the year to one of Shakespeare's or Jonson's" [9] Certainly the preponderance of evidence indicates beyond a doubt that the bulk of the plays of Beaumont and Fletcher, chiefly comedies and tragicomedies, were more popular than those of Jonson.

The possibility of traditional popularity must not be overlooked. Charles the Second was only twelve years old when the the theaters closed in 1642, yet his taste for dramatic entertainments had been formed early. Many of the members of the Restoration audiences and several of the playwrights had lived during the flourishing times of the Jacobeans, and carried with them

[9] Blount, *"De Re Poetica,"* p. 23.

memories of popular plays. We should expect that many of these older courtiers, following the King's wish that the twelve years of the Commonwealth should be regarded as if they never had existed would apply the same reasoning to the theatres. And there can be no doubt of the popularity of Beaumont and Fletcher before 1642.

From the fragments of Sir Henry Herbert's records we find that at court, during the season of 1636-7, thirteen plays were presented. Of these seven were by Beaumont and Fletcher, one by Shakespeare and none by Jonson. Other plays during this season, at which the king (and presumably the prince) was present, numbered nine, of which five were by Beaumont and Fletcher, one, *The Silent Woman*, by Jonson, and two by Shakespeare. The most popular plays of Beaumont and Fletcher were: *The Elder Brother, A King and No King, The Bloody Brother, Cupid's Revenge, A Wife for a Month, Wit Without Money, Philaster, The Coxcomb, The Beggars' Bush, The Maid's Tragedy, The Loyal Subject,* and *Love's Pilgrimage*. Many of these were as popular after the Restoration.

A significant entry of January 6, 1641/2 is worth quoting:

> On Twelfe Night, 1641, the prince had a play called The Scornful Lady [by Beaumont and Fletcher] at the Cockpitt, but the King and Queene were not there; and it was the only play acted at court in the whole Christmas.[10]

At such an anxious time as this Charles, whose later influence on the stage was large, amused himself with Beaumont and Fletcher's great comedy.

Nor was the popularity of the Beaumont and Fletcher dramas lost even after the close of the theatres. Professor Sprague has cited the production of

[10] Adams, op. cit. p. 58.

The Scornful Lady in 1647, of *A King and No King* in the same year, of *Wit Without Money* in 1648 and again in 1654, and of *The Bloody Brother* in 1648, all, of course, clandestine and illegal revivals.[11]   There were also the "drolls" of which twenty-seven were collected in Francis Kirkman's *The Wits, or Sport Upon Sport*. Of these, fourteen are adapted from plays by Beaumont and Fletcher, two from Shakespeare and one from Jonson, a further indication of the overwhelming popularity of the two Jacobeans.[12]

As a final point in our study of relative popularity, let us consider a cross-section of the Restoration stage in the dramatic season of 1661-2.   During this time there were at least nine performances of eight plays by Shakespeare, forty-one of twenty-one by Beaumont and Fletcher, and ten of three by Jonson.   There were also at least twenty-eight revivals of nineteen plays by other of the older dramatists, chiefly Jacobean.   One wonders, in view of these figures, if there were no new plays produced at all, for there must have been other, unrecorded performances of old plays.   Certainly there were very few new plays.   Eighty-eight performances, in nine months or less of acting time, during a period when the theatres were never sure of opening their doors the next day, would certainly bulk large, even with two theatres.   And nearly half of these eighty-eight performances are of plays by Beaumont and Fletcher.

In closet popularity Beaumont and Fletcher lead also.   The lists of quartos and folios of the works of the three major dramatists show that the great Jacobeans were reprinted more often than their contemporaries.

[11] Sprague, A. C., *Beaumont and Fletcher on The Restoration Stage*, p. 3.
[12] *Ibid.* p. 4.

The Critical Attitude

But the evidences of popularity, while important and interesting in themselves, are far from settling the question of relative influences. Another important aspect of the question is that of the critical opinions of the three, as held by Restoration writers. References to and comparisons between the preceding age and the Restoration, by critics and dramatists of the latter period, show that Jonson was regarded as the pattern for dramatists, "the greatest man of the last age," and the man who reformed both the English language and the English stage! Dryden examines *The Silent Woman* at length, as a pattern of dramatic excellence, with reference especially to the Aristotelian unities.[13] Edward Phillips notes of Jonson that:

In three of his comedies, namely *The Fox, Alchemist,* and *Silent Woman,* he may be compared, in the judgment of learned men, for decorum, language and well humoring of parts, as well with the chief of the Greek and Latin comedians as the prime of modern Italians . . . nor is his *Bartholomew Fair* much short of them.[14]

Dryden, the dean of Restoration critics, also speaks of this decorum and exactness, and that abiding by the unities which makes Jonson, to him, preferable in judgment above all other poets.[15] And we find Shadwell, a constant admirer of Ben, declaring as his dramatic creed that:

I have endeavoured to represent variety of humors, most of the persons in the play differing in their characters from one another, which was the practise of Ben Johnson, whom I think all dramatic writers ought to imitate though none are like to come near.[16]

Other citations might be multiplied to show that the

[13] *Essay of Dramatic Poetry,* ed. Mitford, 242.
[14] *Theatrum Poetarum* (Edition 1800,) Vol. I, p. 242.
[15] *Defense of an Essay of Dramatic Poesy.* Scott-Saintbury, II, 314.
[16] Preface to *The Sullen Lovers* (1668).

Restoration critics and dramatists, with few exceptions, united in praise of Ben Jonson on three counts:
his learning, his exactness and decorum (i. e. classicism) and less frequently, his "humors."

But discussion of the art of Jonson invariably
dragged in a consideration of Shakespeare and "The
Twins" (as Mr. Saintsbury calls them). Here, running
true to form, the critics unite in their praise of Jonson
as the learned one of the trio, while praising Shakespeare for his natural poetic ability and Beaumont and
Fletcher (or more generally Fletcher alone) for lux-
uriance of wit and invention. There is a certain con-
descension to be felt in the attitude of critics toward
Shakespeare and Fletcher that is lacking in their discussions of Jonson—the sort of attitude appropriate
to gentlemen who recognize Jonson as a scholar, and
who prided themselves upon their own classical
scholarship. Thus Langbaine speaks of the "vener-
able" Shakespeare and the "learned and judicious"
Jonson. However he praises, as usual, Fletcher's wit:

> No man ever understood or drew the passions more lively than
> he and his brisk raillery was so drest, that it rather pleased than
> disgusted the modest part of his audience.[17]

A critical judgment which we find repeated again and
again.

The critics were not original creatures; they accepted with little hesitation the judgment of their predecessors and often copied them verbatim. Edward
Phillips' conclusion in the *Theatrum Poetarum* of
1675 is accepted by Winstanley in 1687 and again by
Blount in 1694. I quote Blount:

> . . . . each excelled in his peculiar way: Ben Johnson in his
> elaborate pains and knowledge of authors, Shakespeare in his
> pure vein of wit and natural poetic height, Fletcher in a courtly
> elegance and gentile familiarity of stile, and withal a wit and

---

[17] *An Account of the English Dramatic Poets*, p. 203.

invention so overflowing that the luxuriant branches thereof
were frequently thought convenient to be lopt off by Mr. Beaumont.[18]

Flecknoe, the earliest of Restoration critics, repeats
the same formula more concisely:

Shakespeare excelled in a natural vein, Fletcher in wit and
Jonson in gravity and ponderousness of style; whose only fault
was that he was too elaborate and had he mixed less erudition
with his plays, they had been more pleasant and delightful than
they are. Comparing him with Shakespeare, you shall see the
difference between nature and art; and with Fletcher the difference between wit and judgment.[19]

Quotations might be multiplied to show how firmly
fixed these judgments were in the minds of Restora-
tions critics and dramatists. We find, for example,
Edward Howard saying in 1673:

> The witty Fletcher and Elaborate Ben
> And Shakespeare had the first dramatic pen.[20]

Francis Kirkman (1662) speaks of the "rare, ingenu-
ous Fletcher" [21] while Margaret Cavendish, Duchess of
Newcastle, deplores her own lack in a couplet:

> The latin phrases I could never tell,
> But Jonson could, which made him write so well.[22]

And Dryden, at the close of the century, repeats the
old platitudes:

> In easy dialogue is Fletcher's praise;
> He moved the mind, but had not power to raise.
> Great Johnson did by strength of judgement please;
> Yet doubling Fletcher's force, he wants his ease.
> In differing talent both adorned their age;
> One for the study, t'other for the stage.[23]

---

[18] Blount, Thomas Pope. *De Re Poetica*, p. 23.
[19] *A Discourse of the English Stage*, cited in *The Jonson Allusion Book*,
p. 322.
[20] *Poems and Essays by a Gentleman of Quality*. J. A. B., 374.
[21] *The English Lovers, Bookseller to the Reader*. J. A. B, 324.
[22] *General Prologue to all Plays*. J. A. B., 325.
[23] *To My Dear Friend Mr. Congreve on His Comedy Called the Double
Dealer*, 1694.

In effect, Dryden may be said to have summarized in his whole body of critical work the general attitude of the Restoration toward its predecessors. He expresses it all rather concisely in the *Defense of the Epilogue.* He would have his contemporaries admire the beauty and heights of Shakespeare, without imitating his carelessness (a kinder word than crudeness). He would have them imitate the "quickness and easiness" of Fletcher, without following his redundancy of style or linguistic inaccuracies. Fletcher's scenes of love were good, but he could never have written a true heroic play—with the models of perfect, honorable women. And Jonson had accuracy of judgment in the ordering of his plots and choice of characters, but—

> But let us not think him a perfect pattern for imitation, except it be in humor; for love, which is the foundation of all comedies in other languages, is scarcely mentioned in any of his comedies; and for humor itself, the poets of this age will be more wary than to imitate the meanness of his persons. Gentlemen will now be entertained with the follies of each other, and though they allow Cobb and Tib to speak properly, yet they are not much pleased with their tankard or with their rags.[24]

This concensus of critical opinion, which praises Jonson most highly of the three, emphasizing his technique, his gravity and learning, which praises Shakespeare for poetry and Fletcher for wit and ingenuity, is not quite in accord with our conclusions anent relative popularity. We should think that he who is most praised would be most popular. Certainly those plays of Jonson which are technically his best, the four great comedies, were popular in the Restoration—yet were they popular because of their exactness and decorum, their gravity and learning? This question does not arise in connection with the other two members of the

[24] *Defense of the Epilogue,* Scott-Saintsbury, IV, p. 242.

triumvirate. The emphasis upon Shakespeare's poetry agrees with the popularity of his tragedies, although one wonders why the romantic comedies escaped presentation. And the "wit and ingenuity" of Fletcher, fitting in as it does with the Restoration demand for those qualities, goes far toward explaining the popularity of Beaumont and Fletcher.

It is questionable whether the foregoing quotations represent the opinions of the playgoers, who are the real moulders of the drama, or those of the critics alone, between whom and the theaters there was constant war. Perhaps the influence of Jonson on dramatic theory was much greater than on dramatic practice. It must be remembered that in the Restoration, Neo-Classicism, urged on by translations from Aristotle, Horace, Longinus and their French followers, was developing rapidly toward its climax in the eighteenth century, and classical dogmas were filtering slowly down through the upper strata of critical erudition.[25] Dryden preached the doctrine of the unities in his *Essay of Dramatic Poesy* (1668) and, although his critical tenets underwent various changes during his lifetime, he remained true, at least in theory, to his early love.[26] Such dramatists as Shadwell and Sir Robert Howard, professed followers of Jonson, also claimed adherence to the best classical principles. Howard admits that he has been converted from an earlier point of view, agreeing:

. . . that our best poets have differed from other nations (though not so happily) in usually mingling and interweaving mirth and sadness through the whole course of their plays, Ben Johnson only excepted, who keeps himself entire to one

[25] For a thorough discussion of classical tendencies see Krutch, J. W., *Comedy and Conscience after the Restoration,* Chapters 3 and 4.

[26] c. f. Bohn, Wm. H. *The Development of John Dryden's Literary Criticism,* P. M. L. A. XXII 1.

argument; and I confess I am now convinced in my own judgment, that it is most proper to keep the audience in one entire
disposition both of concern and attention.[27]

But Howard did not always adhere to his belief, in
practise, at least.

Dryden's appeal to Jonson, in his discussion of the
ancients, always the final authorities on matters of
dramatic law, gives us the key to the situation:

In the meantime, I must desire you to take notice, that the
greatest man of the last age (Jonson) was willing to give place
to them in all things: he was not only a professed imitator of
Horace but a learned plagiary of all the others; you can track
him everywhere in their snow.[28]

Jonson, thus, was looked upon as the intermediary
between the Neo-Classicists and their models. He was
thoroughly in agreement, both in technique and in
critical pronouncements, with the general classicising
tendency. It is only reasonable to suppose that critics
with pre-conceived ideas of excellence will find quality only in that work which has been done according
to their standards. So the Restoration critics approved of Jonson. It is Jonson the classicist, not Jonson the creator of humors, who appealed to them. This
alone is sufficient to account for the constant praise of
the great Ben. And there is also to be taken into account the traditional Jonson of forceful personality,
the fighter, rebel and yet autocrat. So strong was his
personality, so great his weight and strength that, in
spite of the failure of many of his plays when first
presented, his contemporaries, praising them as mas-
terpieces of writing, discreetly overlooked their faults
as acting dramas. This tradition descended to the
Restoration.

However, when we consider the comedies of the
Restoration we must admit that classical dogmas had

---

[27] Introduction to *The Surprisal*, 1665.
[28] *Essay of Dramatic Poesy*, ed. Mitford, p. 227.

little effect until the very close of the period. As Mr. Krutch expresses it, the dramatists:

> . . . bowed to the unities so far as to prune the Elizabethan luxuriance which liked to spread a play over a whole lifetime and move the scenes over the whole face of the earth, and they felt that it was better as a rule to confine scenes to a relatively restricted area and the time to a few days; but they refused to cramp themselves within the twenty-four hours of a natural day, or to follow Rymer's precepts which would have converted the drama into something wholly removed from life.[29]

And, so far as the unity of action is concerned, it is obvious that the most successful Restoration comedies were those which were complicated with the greatest number of intrigues and plots, tangled up in an almost hopeless confusion. Even Dryden, who was, however, always something of a fence-straddler, has his mixtures of humor and romance, and his chaotic, confused plots. And Shadwell, classic example of the Jonsonian follower, dropped into the procession inevitably. But we shall reserve him for a later discussion.

The critics and dramatists were not wholly united in their pleas for decorum and the unities. The numerous prologues and epilogues to the comedies bear witness to the strength and virulence of the constant controversy over dramatic methods. Many writers aligned themselves against classicism. Butler impeached the critics and those who borrowed plots from foreign sources:

> And by an action falsely laid of trover
> The lumber of their proper goods recover
> Enough to furnish all the lewd impeachers
> Of witty Beaumont's poetry and Fletcher's,
> Who for a few misprisions of wit,
> Are charged by those who ten times worse commit;
> And for misjudging some unhappy scenes,
> Are censured for 't with more unlucky sense;
> When all their worse miscarriages delight,
> And please more than the best that pedants write.[30]

---

[29] Krutch, op. cit., p. 68.
[30] Butler, Samuel, *Remains* (col. 1729).

And Farquhar, at the close of the century, launched a notable attack on the unities, concluding:

> I would willingly understand the regularities of "Hamlet," "Macbeth," "Henry IV" and of Fletcher's plays; and yet these have long been the darlings of the English audience, and are like to continue with the same applause in defiance of all the criticisms that were ever published in Greek and Latin. . . . What a misfortune it is to these gentlemen [the critics] to be natives of such an ignorant, self-willed, impertinent island, where let a critic and scholar find never so many irregularities in a play yet five hundred saucy people will come to see the play forty and fifty times in a year.[31]

If Restoration comedy itself was only to a degree influenced by classicism and yet Restoration criticism was decidedly classical, and if the critics, as we have seen, referred to Jonson as an authority, we can only conclude that his influence must have been upon the critics rather than the dramatists. Lip-service there certainly was, but the contents of the plays are of more importance than anything written about those plays. Reserving, then, our consideration of the Beaumont and Fletcher types for a later chapter, let us consider, from an examination of Restoration comedy, the drama of Shakespeare and that of Jonson, what parallels there may be between the new comedy and these examples of the old, in spirit, technique, plots, characters, wit and humor.

[31] *A Discourse Upon Comedy*, quoted in Durham, *Critical Essays of the Eighteenth Century*, p. 259.

Chapter II

JONSON, SHAKESPEARE AND THE
RESTORATION

Jonson

RESTORATION COMEDY has been known for genera-
tions only by the work of the chief writers of the
"manners" school. As far as excellence is concerned,
the works of Congreve, Wycherley, Farquhar, Vanbrugh and Etherege are undoubtedly most important
to us today, but it must be remembered that the five
dramatists wrote all together only thirty plays. Some
of these were failures on the stage, notably *The Way
of the World,* and some, produced well along in the
eighteenth century, are out of our period. D'Urfey,
with twenty comedies, Mrs. Behn and Shadwell with
thirteen each, Dryden with eight comedies, Crowne
with five, and Ravenscroft with eight, a total of sixty-
seven, provided far more actual entertainment than
the five writers whose work is usually considered all of
Restoration comedy. And many minor playwrights,
each with one to four comedies to his credit, forgotten now but important in their day, must also be considered. If we are to lump together Restoration
comedy as a whole, we must consider what situations,
characters, dramatic methods and attitudes are most
characteristic of the entire group. To characterize it
all by *The Way of the World* would be to arrive at a
picture far from the truth; yet the kinship of spirit
between this, the finest of sophisticated comedies, and
any of the minor plays of farce and intrigue, is obvious on comparison. The same ideas, stock situations,
and characters which are used in the comedies of

manners, appear in different and usually coarser garb in the great bulk of the drama.

In the sum total of this comedy there are various mixtures of love-intrigue, romance, realism, satire and farce. We cannot say that any one writer represents in all his work, even in one play, any one strain to the exclusion of the remainder. Nor is it possible to say that any one writer kept in general to one strain. Mrs. Behn, to take an example, turns to farce in *The Feign'd Curtezans*, romantic love in *The Forc'd Marriage,* and satire in *The Roundheads.* Occasionally she may make use of realism or romance, yet sophistication with her, as with all other dramatists of the period, is paramount, and sex intrigue is her chief theme. Dryden mixes intrigue with romance in *The Spanish Friar*, deals almost wholly with realism and satire in *Limberham*, combines romance and intrigue in *The Rival Ladies*, and, in short, has no one comedy that can be classed completely under one heading. Even in Congreve, Wycherley and Etherege we find mixtures. *The Comical Revenge,* by the last writer, so often hailed as the first of typical Restoration comedies, combines two plots, one of intrigue and farce, the other of high romance, near-tragic in tone. *The Man of the Mode* is satiric (manners) and yet based on intrigue. So with *She Would if She Could, The Way of the World, The Gentleman Dancing Master, The Relapse,* and others of the type usually called comedy of manners.

Fundamentally the great majority of Restoration comedies are based upon love and sex intrigue,—love rarely honorable, usually illicit, and not infrequently preverted. This was in agreement with the life of the period, when the pursuit of women was the chief occupation of all the men of Charles' court, from the king down. In the comedy of manners, too, if we accept Mr.

Nicoll's definition of that type of comedy as characterized by:

..the presence of at least one pair of witty lovers, the woman
as emancipated as the man, their dialogue free and graceful,
an air of refined cynicism over the whole production, the plot of
less consequence than the wit, an absence of crude realism, a
total lack of any emotion whatever.

sex was important, and an analysis of any typical
comedy of manners reveals the fact that the intrigue
is usually of the illicit variety. What the Restoration
wanted in its plays was a mixture of qualities,[2] but it
particularly loved two; wit, by which it meant raillery
and repartee, always bordering upon the verge of the
unmentionable, and a good, lively plot, full of action,
surprises, mistaken identities, fights, bedroom scenes
and the like.

The popular types of characters fitted in with this
general desire. The witty lovers (sometimes not so
witty)—a gentleman, reckless, swaggering, swearing,
prodigal and whoring, and a lady, careless of everything but her reputation, are present in all of the best
and most of the second best comedies. A confidant
for each, a cuckolded husband or two, a heavy father,
uncle, or guardian, a few low comedy characters, conceived in something approaching the spirit of the Jonsonian "humors" characters, and the dramatis personae is fairly complete. These are the theatrical
types of the Restoration and they are used over and
over again, frequently with only the names altered.

In the same way stock situations and plots appear
and re-appear. By far the most common deals with
the two lovers, of whom the lady is either scornful of

---

[1] Nicoll, Allardyce, *Restoration Drama*, p. 185.

[2] Farquhar, *A Discourse Upon Comedy*, Durham, op. cit., p. 259. "The
scholar calls upon us for Decorum and Oeconommy; the courtier cries out
for wit and purity of stile; the citizen for humor and ridicule; the divines
threaten us for immodesty; and the ladies will have an intreague."

her lover, affectedly coy, or shut up by some parent or guardian. In the last case the play concerns itself with the lover's attempts to gain access to his mistress by disguising himself as a monk, a barber, a dancing master, a near relative, a woman, or what-not; or he may attempt to carry her away by force or stratagem. If the object of the young man's affections is married the story is still further complicated by the arrival of the husband at the sudden and physiological moment. The stock low comedy characters (of whom the husband is usually one), the fop, the coward, the braggart, the would-be wit, or poet, or man of fashion, are manipulated in much the same lively satirical fashion, and placed in situations in which their affectations of manner and dress may be most advantageously developed. The fop invariably struts and preens his plumes, and is usually ducked in a puddle; the coward is beaten, the wit humiliated, the poet lampooned and the husband cuckolded.

A long list of common situations might be drawn up: the woman hater brought to his knees, [3] the woman disguised as a man, following her lover, fighting duels, or making love to another women, the lover using artifice and trickery to make his mistress declare her love for him, [5] cross-purpose marriages, in which one or both parties is deceived, [6] and a dozen others.

If we mix up an olla podrida of type characters and type situations, dependent upon an intrigue plot, and conceived in a devil-may-care spirit of light immoral-

[3] References follow to a few typical plays in which the situations are used. Many more might be cited. D'Urfey, *Marriage Hater Match'd*, Johnson, *The Country Lasses*, Farquhar, *The Constant Couple*, Mrs. Behn, *The Rover*, Otway, *The Atheist*.

[4] Granville, *The She-Gallants*, Wycherley, *The Plain Dealer*, Farquhar, *The Inconstant*, Shadwell, *Bury Fair*.

[5] Congreve, *Love for Love*, Etherege, *Comical Revenge*.

[6] Farquhar, *Love and a Bottle*, Congreve *Love for Love*, Shadwell *The Humorists*, D'Urfey *The Fool Turn'd Critic*.

ity, which is often downright obscenity, we have what
may be called a typical Restoration comedy. Place the
emphasis chiefly upon particularized satire of contemporary people and manners, done cynically and wit-
tily, and we have the comedy of manners. But serious
satire for reformatory purposes, serious characterization, or truly moral observations must not be allowed
to creep in. Any sentiment must be of the most meretricious sort, and used for base ends, while real emotion, if introduced at all, must be used as a butt for
laughter, unless, of course, a romantic sub-plot is used.
Even in the latter, however, there is always the element of artificiality.

If we examine the comedies of Jonson, we find that
so far as basic themes are concerned, they have little
in common with the Restoration. With the love motif
Jonson would have nothing to do.[7] *The Case is Altered,* the only play in which he deals at all with romance, was not acknowledged by him, was not printed
with his works, and was unknown to the Restoration.
Even, in this play, however, we are not dealing with
love as the later dramatists, or as Beaumont and
Fletcher treated it; sex is kept down to a minimum,
and the love of Paulo Fernese for Rachel is perfectly
honest and idylic. Angelo, who, a generation later,
would have been the hero of the play, is made a villian
by Jonson. Where the dramatist elsewhere occasionally deals with intrigue, sketchily to be sure, his
ubiquitous morality leads him far away from Restoration conclusions. Wittypole and Mrs. Fitzdotterel, in
The Devil is an Ass, are no cynical, emancipated lovers;
they reform honestly before their intrigue has been
carried to its logical conclusion. Dryden was wise in
forbidding his generation to follow Jonson in the writ-

[7] Cf. Kerr, Mina, *The Influence of Ben Jonson on Comedy* 1598-1642, p. 9.

ing of love scenes, for Jonson has none worthy of the name.

The four great plays, so often presented in the Restoration, *Bartholomew Fair, The Alchemist, The Silent Woman,* and *Volpone,* splendid examples of rare dramatic types that hardly admit of imitation, were popular not because of their similarity to the later comedy, but in spite of their lack of such similarity.[8] *Bartholomew Fair,* formless and chaotic, has no resemblance to any Restoration comedy, and must have pleased because of two things: the satire on the Puritans,[9] and the scenes of farce, notably that of the puppet show (in spite of Pepys' dislike for this kind of entertainment). *"Bartholomew Fair,"* Mr. Symonds concludes, "is a pure farce, conceived in the spirit of rollicking mirth and executed with colossal energy." [19] How far is such a statement from a description of the Restoration sophisticated comedy!

The Alchemist and *Volpone,* similar to each other in some ways, are also divided from the Restoration by a wide gulf. Both are typical of the Jonsonian philosophy which divided the world into two classes, the gullers and the gulled. Both are serious comedies, verging on the boundaries of tragedy. Neither deals with love, unless, indeed, the monstrous lust of Volpone may be so called; and while neither is strikingly moral, yet they are decidedly not salacious. They must have pleased the jaded tastes of the later audiences

[8] The statement of Thomas Davies, although later, is pertinent. *Dramatic Miscellanies,* 1783, 392: "A taste for Johnson was endeavoured to be revived (in the Restoration) though, I believe, that was always an uphill work."

[9] Herford and Simpson, *Ben Jonson,* II, 131. "The lively satire of the Puritans had probably as large a share in its success on the stage they disparaged, as its brilliant rendering of the amenities of the famous London fair. . . After the Restoration it was promptly brought out of hiding, and its polemical salt helped to preserve a piece which flagrantly contravened in many points the new tendencies of the drama."

[10] Symonds, J. A., *Ben Jonson,* p. 111.

by their pictures of strange and unusual crimes, their horrible exaggerations of personified vices, and the relentless unfolding of unusual plots. And while *The Silent Woman*, held up by Dryden as the model of a perfect comedy, may have owed much of its success to the critical puffs it received, much more was probably due to its complexity and skillful plot development. But these are plays which might easily succeed on the stage today; they are practically timeless and have little to do with the changing fashions of the theatre. Certainly, however, if we look in them for love intrigue, for wit and raillery, for immorality, emancipated women, and gay, sophisticated rakes, in short, for the typical ideas, characters and situations of Restoration comedy, we shall be disappointed.

The Case is Altered, Cynthia's Revels, The New Inn, The Magnetic Lady, Poetaster, The Staple of the News and *The Tale of a Tub* have left no records of any appearance on the Restoration stage, except, of course, their inclusion in the original play-lists at the first revival of the theaters. *The Devil is an Ass, Everyman In His Humor* and *Everyman Out of His Humor*, must have appeared at rare intervals, for Downes and Langbaine both mention them. For the seven of Jonson's comedies that were produced at all, I can list a total number of only ninety-seven recorded performances, spread over a period of sixty years, a sufficiently small number to cause us to doubt Jonson's popularity.

Surprisingly enough none of the comedies was altered during the Restoration period. This may have been the result of the universal critical praise of Jonson. To have altered the work of the master would have been an act of apostasy. More probably, however, the failure to alter one of the four popular comedies was due to the inability or unwillingness of

anyone to undertake such a stupendous task. To have
added, say, an intrigue to *The Silent Woman* would
have meant the revision of the entire play, and endless
work fitting together the great, intricate plot, now
with a new set of incompatible wheels. And the failure to raid the storehouse of Jonson's minor comedies,
as that of many another old dramatist was raided, was
probably due to the fact that there were so few jewels
there.   How could it have been possible to alter
Cynthia's Revels to the liking of a later-day audience?
The play is an allegory, practically plotless, learned,
moral, packed with wisdom; there is nothing upon
which a later dramatist could lay hold. And so with
his other plays—the long parades of "humor" characters, the lack of an interesting plot (the first re-
quisite for the reviser) the allegorys, the morality, the
tedious conversations on esoteric subjects, were excellent watch-dogs over the treasury of plays. And the
borrowing of amusing situations, so common with
Restoration writers, was forbidden by the fact that so
few of Jonson's situations are amusing, or could have
been, at least, amusing to the Restoration.   *The Tale
of a Tub,* for example, a decidedly funny low comedy
of country life, must have clashed with the Restoration
hatred for country life and country themes.

Differences in the matter of plot structure are strikingly apparent.   Jonson's plots, in his greater comedies, are marvels of intricate, careful workmanship;
so exact is the dove-tailing of each element that the
plays often seem machine made. And, while they must
have appealed to the Restoration from time to time,
it is certainly true that the daily fare of that period
was far different.   The Restoration loved diversity
and surprises—it cared little for protasis and epitasis,

catastasis and catastrophe.   Scholarly learning and
scholarly practise the audiences suspected equally.[11]
In the typical late seventeenth century comedies intrigues may come to a climax in the third act and new
intrigues begin in the fourth; the title or chief character, much as in the modern style, may not be introduced until the middle of the play; incidents and
dialogues are piled upon each other in bewildering and
almost Caroline confusion.   Again, in many of Jonson's minor comedies, *Cynthia's Revels* and *The Magnetic Lady* for example, the plot does not develop until
the last act, the first four being taken up with the
delineation of manners.   Needless to say, with the
exception of a rare comedy of manners, or two, this
method finds no parallels in the Restoration.

In spirit, too, there is a strong contrast.   Jonson, in
whom the spirit of indignation bubbled up in bitter
satire, looked on the world as a vast near-tragic farce.
His satire is directed against every abuse, every affection—one is almost inclined to say against
everything and everyone, so inclusive it is.   A few rare
and shadowy "good" characters he has: Dame Pliant,
for example, in *The Alchemist* which contains otherwise the whole category of rogues.   The purity of
Celia stands out sharply against a world of villians in
Volpone; The Silent Woman and *Bartholomew Fair*
have their degrees of roguery and folly, but there is
hardly a character with whom we feel called upon to
sympathize.   As Mr. Nicoll has pointed out:

There is always a certain vulgarity in true satire; and there
is always a sense that the poet before writing has looked into his

[11] Mrs. Behn, Preface to *The Dutch Lover*: "Plays have no room for that
which is men's great advantage over women, that is learning. . . We
all know that the immortal Shakespeare's plays. . . have better pleased
the world than Jonson's works. . . and it hath been observed that they are
apt to admire him most confoundedly who have just such a scantling of it
as Johnson had."

own heart. He is horrified at the vices he sees in himself. This note is deeply stressed in Jonson's plays; it is apparent in Swift; and it occurs in a very marked form in Wycherley's "The Plain Dealer." [12]

This is not the satire which we feel in the commonalty of Restoration comedies. Where Jonson satirized vice and folly, the Restoration satirized only folly: that is, foppishness, affectations of speech, manner and dress, surface rather than fundamental characteristics. And where Jonson satirized nearly all sorts and conditions of men, the Restoration picked on certain definite types as fair game, dividing its dramatis personae into two groups, the baiters and the baited. The "humor" characters, those generally satirized, were reserved for the low comedy parts. Sir Courtly Nice is a minor character in Crowne's play by that name; Sir Fopling Flutter is brought into Etherege's *The Man of Mode* as a butt for the jokes of the company; Sir Timothy Tawdry in Mrs. Behn's *The Town Fop* is a slap-stick clown. There is much laughter and but little bitterness in Restoration comedy.

And if the Restoration could have little sympathy for Jonson's learning, even while pretending to admire it, still less sympathy could it have for his morality and relative cleanliness—i.e. freedom from bawdry. Wit for its own sake, obscenity merely for the pleasure of being obscene, the insinuation which is more indecent than the broadest vulgarity, the rewarding of the wicked and the neglect, if not chastising, of the good—these are the things prized in the upside-down world of Restoration comedy. We find a dozen dramatists giving lip-service to morality, alleging, as their defence against the militant Collier, their desire to reform the age, but we know as we read that they do

[12] Nicoll, Allardyce, *Introduction to Dramatic Theory*, 175.

not mean it. With the classical dictum that the aim of comedy is to instruct as well as to give pleasure, they had little to do.

There remains one possible source of Jonsonian influence: the so-called "humors." A great deal has been said upon this subject in the prefaces to seventeenth century comedies, and more in recent criticism.[13] There can be no doubt that much of this dramatic method was carried down to the Restoration, partly through Jonson's plays and critical utterances, and partly through the medium of Beaumont and Fletcher, Shakespeare, Brome, Shirley, and others who fell partly or wholly under Jonson's influence. But the tendency has been to see in every well developed dramatic character a "humors" character, and there are hosts of figures in Restoration comedy who have nothing to do with "humors." We must recognize that this word meant with Jonson, in effect, a caricature of an individual, a sublimation of his traits to the result that he might appear dominated by one only.[14] As a result we have Morose, Face, Subtle, Volpone, Corbaccio, Justice Over-do, and the dozens of other Jonsonian characters, whose names, actions and personalities are exaggerations of one characteristic. To claim for this method a complete influence upon seventeenth century comedy is itself an exaggeration. One would hesitate to call the Falstaff of *Henry IV, 1* a caricature, just as one hesitates to apply the same term to the Vainloves, Valentines, Armintas and Be-

[13] Nicoll, Allardyce, *Restoration Drama*, p. 189: "Jonson was the first great classicist in our drama, and in his humors he succeeded in stamping his impress heavily and securely on all later dramatic endeavour."

[14] A true humor is:
"As when some one peculiar quality
Doth so possess a man that it doth draw
All his affects, his spirits and his powers
In their confluctions all to run one way."
—Prologue to *Every Man in His Humor*.

lindas of the Restoration. In the comedy of manners, certainly, we should expect to see the greatest use made of this method, for this type of comedy it was which dealt most with satire. Yet, although humors are present, they are not of the Jonsonian flavor. Artificialized the characters are, assuredly, and many of them are dominated, to some extent at least, by mannerisms, conventional formulas and the like, but that is a very different matter.[15]

However, in a few plays, avowed imitations of Jonson's comedies, we see the "humors" method carried out entirely. Shadwell's Virtuoso, Stanford, Goldingham, the miser, his Kestrils, Hackwells, Sir Formals and Watchums are certainly conceived and executed in this manner. So, too, with many other characters, chiefly minor, in the works of other playwrights. Sir John Daw and Sir Amorous La-foole are in many ways the ancestors of Sir Joseph Wittol, in Congreve's *The Old Bachelor,* and Sir Simon Addleplot, in Wycherley's *Love in a Wood,* to mention two only, while the sharpers, fops, bullies, cowards, affected ladies and gentlemen of all kinds bear a not too distant resemblance to the Jonsonian types. But we must recognize the fact that Jonson rarely attempted, as did the Restoration writers, to delineate the refinements and delicacies of social life on a higher plane, preferring

---

[15] Nicoll, Allardyce, *Introduction to Dramatic Theory,* p. 186. "There may be 'humors' in the plays of Etherge, Congreve, Farquhar and Vanbrugh, but those "humors' are not stressed to the same extent as they are in Jonson's work; and there is, moreover, a marked change in the conception. In Jonson, as we have seen, the 'humors' are exaggerated traits of character. In the comedy of manners on the other hand, the 'humors' are rarely such traits of character exaggerated. The humors, if we retain the old term, are derived from the conventions, follies and usages of social life. Greed is not much represented in the comedy of manners, but it is in Jonson's plays, precisely because greed is a trait of character, not a quality derived from social custom." It is a bit difficult to reconcile this with the statement by the same author, ante, p. 31n.

the "colloquial barbarisms" of Ursula, the pig woman, Sir Epicure Mammon, and Brainworm. And while characters of this low comedy type appear in numbers in the later comedy, the chief personages of the plays remain true to the types inherited from Beaumont and Fletcher and elaborated upon by the Restoration into artificial but lively and interesting ladies and gentlemen.

To see more concretely the status of satire and humors in the Restoration let us pick at random a comedy which will be nearly typical. Here is Otway's *Friendship in Fashion,* a play which combines intrigue, wit, satire and farce. The story is:

Goodvile has debauched Victoria, and to get rid of her plans to marry her to his bosom friend, Trueman, while at the same time he is making love to Camilla, mistress of Valentine, another close friend. As a result he is deceived by his wife and cuckolded by Trueman. Camilla misleads him and marries Valentine; Victoria, as a last resort, marries Sir Noble Clumsy, one of the low comedy characters, and Trueman and Mrs. Goodvile are left to enjoy their illicit love unpunished.

The poet directs his satire, not at Goodvile or Trueman, as Jonson would, but at Malagene, Caper, Saunter, Sir Noble Clumsy and Lady Squeamish, harmless, affected creatures, whose names are the signs of their dispositions. These characters are conceived in something akin to the "humors" spirit, but again with the important difference that it is rather exaggerated affectations of manner, speech and dress that are attacked, than characteristic traits. With the leading characters, a group of reckless, immoral, witty people, with whom the audience must have had much in common, we feel that we are called upon to sympathize; certainly none of them is punished. Goodvile does not even lose the friendship of the two men whom he tried to victimize. This is the sort of thing that was done by the Restoration dramatists; its differences from the Jonsonian drama are apparent.

Of the possible imitators of Jonson in the Restoration, Edward Howard, Shadwell, John Wilson, and possibly Robert Howard, are the best known. Of these, Shadwell and Edward Howard were the most emphatic in their praise of Jonson and their avowals of his mastership. Yet they present some strange paradoxes in their work. In Howard's *The Six Day's Adventure*, the main plot has much in common with that of Fletcher's *The Sea Voyage*, while the most important sub-plot is a re-working of the theme of Jonson's *The Silent Woman*. According to Howard's admission in the preface to the play, it was a failure on the stage. His *The Women's Conquest* is even stranger. After a first prologue, on the Jonsonian model of an antecedent discussion of the play between actors, there comes on, in a second prologue, the spirit of Jonson, who threatens to castigate the audience for deserting his ways in drama. [16] In a third prologue the author modestly admits that he has tried to write in the style of Jonson. Yet the play proves to be a tragi-comedy of romantic eroticism, in the typical Fletcherian manner, with not a suggestion of Jonson about it. There are only two possible explanations of such a perverse paradox: one that the writer did not know Jonson, which is certainly dubious, or that he merely fell into the common form of lip worship in his prologues, (which may not have been given on the stage) and in his play gave the audience what it wanted. His own statement in the preface is that the play was a success.

Now if we consider Shadwell, commonly mentioned as the chief imitator of Jonson, we can see still more clearly the difference between preachment and prac-

---

[16] Significantly, the tone of all these Jonsonian followers is usually one of lamentation that the ways of Jonson have been deserted by the stage.

tise. For, although Shadwell undoubtedly started out
with the sincere intention of imitating his Jacobean
master, and was always to some extent under his influence, yet the pressure of the audience and the contemporary method was too great for him to withstand.
He was the author of nineteen plays: two tragedies,
(one an alteration of *Timon of Athens*) one tragi-
comedy, two dramatic operas, (one an alteration of the
long-suffering *The Tempest*) and thirteen comedies.
The one original tragedy, *The Libertine*, tells us
nothing. It is certainly not classic in form. The story
of Don Juan and his escapades, it is formless and episodic. The dramatic operas are in an entirely new
method and show only contemporary influences. The
one tragi-comedy,[17] *The Royal Shepherdess*, is full
of Fletcherian reminiscences. The main plot, dealing
with the love of the king of Arcadia for a lady of supposedly low birth, suggests Beaumont and Fletcher's
A Wife for a Month and *The Humorous Lieutenant*. The situation in which the king's beloved is the
mistress of the king's son, now absent at war, is strikingly paralleled in *The Humorous Lieutenant*. There
are suggestions also, in style and method, of *The Two
Noble Kinsmen*, and *The Maid's Tragedy*. The
whole treatment of the play is typical of the love and
honor type of tragi-comedy, romantic and erotic, which
was set in motion by Beaumont and Fletcher, and carried on by such men as Davenant and Dryden, chiefly.

In comedy proper, Shadwell made known his dramatic precepts and prejudices in the preface to his
first play, *The Sullen Lovers*.

Though I have known some of late so insolent as to say
that Ben Johnson wrote his best plays without wit, imagining
that all the wit in plays consisted in bringing two persons upon

[17] Mr. Nicoll erroneously calls this a pastoral. *Restoration Drama*, p. 192.

the stage to break jests and to bob one another, which they call
repartie; not considering that there is more wit and invention
required in the finding out good humor and matter proper for it
than in all their smart reparties. For in the writing of humor,
a man is confined not to swerve from the character, and obliged
to say nothing but what is proper to it: but in the plays, which
have been wrote of late, there is no such thing as a perfect
character, but the two chief persons are most commonly a swearing, drinking, whoring ruffian for a lover, and an impudent, ill-
bred tomrig for a mistress, and these are the fine people of the
play; and there is that latitude in this: that almost anything is
proper for them to say; but their chief subject is bawdy and profaneness, which they call brisk writing.

Truly this is a worthy declaration, and an apt characterization of the contemporary drama. Had the
dramatist lived up to his first ideals, he might have
deserved the name of son to the great Ben. But Shadwell, although by nature fitted to be a censor of morals
and manners, lacked the fine strength of his Jacobean
master, which made the latter stick to his principles
in spite of the opposition of fellow playwrights and the
London audiences. His first comedies, *The Sullen
Lovers, The Humorists,* and *The Miser* are full
of the Jonsonian manner. But after these three, Shadwell drifted gradually away, and with *Epsom Wells*
in 1672, he arrived in the mainstream of Restoration
intrigue-manners comedy. Although he was never
free of the Jonsonian influence, his later plays represent an almost complete renunciation of his earlier
ideals. In his heavy manner he took up Restoration
wit with a will and "broke jests" and "bobbed" with
the best. The Restoration bawdy became vulgarity
with him and some of his plays are decidedly obscene.
The double-entendre and the cynical jest on sacred subjects are to be found in the pages of most of his later
work. And as for "swearing, drinking, whoring ruf-
fians" and "impudent, ill-bred tom-rigs," the objects of

his earlier scorn, we need only point to Lucindo and
Doristeo, Elvira and Rosaino, in *The Amorous Bigot*
(1690), to Wildish and Bellamy, Gertrude and Phila-
delphia, in *Bury Fair*, (1689) to Raines and Bevil,
Caroline and Lucia, in *Epsom Wells*, (1672) to Sir
Will Rant and Wildfire, Eugenia and Clara, in *The
Scowrers* (1690), and to Bellamour and Carlos, Isabella and Theodosia, in *A True Widow*, (1679).
Even in *The Humorists*, (1670) where, if anywhere,
the influence of Jonson is most apparent, love intrigue
forms the background of the play: disguises, mistaken
marriages, cuckoldings, true and false love. In most
of his plays it is also true that the classical unities are
but weakly adhered to; the unity of action, especially,
is buried beneath an avalanche of plots and counter-
plots, in true Restoration style.

A brief analysis of Shadwell's *Epsom Wells*, perhaps his best comedy, will illustrate how far he drifted
from Jonson. To extricate the threads of intrigue is
highly difficult. We have one hero, Raines, who is
loved by two citizens' wives, Mrs. Bisket, his mistress,
and Mrs. Fribble. With his friend Bevil, he meets two
ladies, Caroline and Lucia. The four promptly fall
into witty and suggestive love making. Bevil has as
his mistress Mrs. Woodly, whose husband is endeavoring to seduce Caroline. Into this confusion comes
Clodpate, a "humors" character, who hates London,
Jilt, a ladies' maid who endeavors to capture Clodpate
in a matrimonial net, two scoundrels, Kick and Cuff,
and the cuckolded citizens, Bisket and Fribble. The
plot comprises a series of amorous adventures, termi-
nating in the divorce of the Woodlys, the capture of
the citizens' wives in adultery by their husbands, the
capture and freeing of Clodpate, by Jilt, and the ac-
ceptance of the two gentlemen, Raines and Bevil, as

lovers, object matrimony, by the two ladies. Of Jonsonian characters the only suspicions are Clodpate and the two citizens, who are much more Middletonian. Of Jonsonian ideas there are none. Indecency, cynicism and wit predominate. There is, however, some realism, and some satire directed at the habitues of a watering place.

Shadwell's fall from grace is a typical illustration of the well known fact that a dramatist must give an audience what it wants. Whatever his desires may have been, if he was to be a successful writer he was obliged to fall in with the intrigue tradition, — his least successful plays were his "humors" comedies —, and Shadwell, primarily a man of the theatre, showed his easy adaptability by beating his contemporaries at their own game. The audiences wanted clever intrigue, sex, immorality and wit, — he gave them all they asked and added perversions to thicken the mixture.

It is doubtful if a true follower of Jonson could have been successful in the Restoration. Wilson, with two such close imitations as *The Cheats* (1663) and *The Projectors* (unacted?) seems to have made very little stir in his world. Sir Robert Howard's play, *The Committee* is often mentioned, erroneously I think, as a typical "humors" comedy. It is one of the first comedies in the Restoration to make use of the new characters of the wild gallant and his opposite, the witty, emancipated lady, in an intrigue plot which carries the burden of a political satire. The "humors" element is subordinate to the intrigue and manners characters. Of such minor dramatists as Lacy, Cavendish, Rawlins, and others, it is hardly necessary to speak. Their work belongs to the realm of farce, where Jonson's influence is unquestionable.

To summarize, it is evident that the comedies of the Restoration differed from those of Jonson in a number of important respects, (but always with a few noted exceptions.)

1. In subject matter the two groups are unquestionably far apart, — Jonson scorning the plots and themes which were dearest to the hearts of later audiences.

2. In dramatic technique, the only relationship lies in a tendency to bring the Restoration somewhat closer to classic traditions, however, never arriving at complete classicism.   And this influence Jonson must share with others.

3. Stock characters and situations peculiar to Jonson are relegated generally to the regions of low comedy and farce.   And an entirely different set of chief personages, unknown to Jonson, occupy the important parts.

4. In spirit there could be no relationship between the moral satirist, Jonson (or occasionally the ebullient Elizabethan) and the cynical, immoral gentlemen of the court of Charles II.

5. The one possible influence is that of the "humors" method of characterization, and that must be confined mainly to the rather narrow field of farce.[18]

Shakespeare

The problem of Shakespeare's possible influence is relatively much simpler.   His comedies were, for the most part, neglected by the Restoration stage.   It is a bit difficult to see why *Love's Labour's Lost, The Two Gentlemen of Verona, The Comedy of Errors, The Winter's Tale, All's Well That Ends Well,* and *Much Ado*

---

[18] Further proof that the "humors" method had a relatively small affect on the Restoration may be found in the unpopularity of *Everyman in His Humor* and *Everyman Out of His Humor,* two comedies in which this method receives its best exposition.

About Nothing should have never appeared.   Mr.
Nicoll's belief that "in the early comedies there is too
much romance and in the later too chaotic plots" [19]
seems to be rather untenable.   I suggest instead that
in the romantic comedies the romance was of a type
which did not appeal to the Restoration—that is, emo-
tional, fairy-like romance, lacking in eroticism and
exaggerated passion—while in the comedies the humor
was too clean for later day tastes.   We should have
expected, for example, that *Much Ado About Nothing*
having a pair of lovers, Benedick and Beatrice, who
are in many ways close to their later prototypes, would
have been highly popular.   But their fun—and surely
they are a pair of witty, emancipated people, highly
sophisticated—is clean, normal and natural, lacking
in the cynical bawdry which distinguishes the speech
of later lovers.   Significantly when Davenant composed
a rificamento of *Measure for Measure* and *Much Ado
About Nothing,* it was the plot dealing with the lovers
which he took from the latter comedy.   But his new
production had no lasting success.

Those comedies which appeared in the Restoration
were usually altered.   The fairy romance of *The Tempest* was turned into broad farce.   *The Taming of the
Shrew* was broadened and coarsened.   *Midsummer
Night's Dream* was made into an opera; while *Cymbeline* was greatly exaggerated and made more sentimental.   *The Merchant of Venice* does not seem to
have appeared until it came upon the stage, altered,
in 1701.   *The Merry Wives of Windsor* appeared
briefly, unaltered, as did *Twelfth Night,* but both were
revised by the beginning of the next century.   Only a
few of the tragedies maintained the stage unaltered,
but their popularity must have been enormous.

[19] Nicoll, Allardyce, *Restoration Drama,* p. 162.

Professor Lounsbury's comparison between the Shakespearian and Fletcherian comedies is enlightening as to the reasons for the popularity of the latter rather than the former:

> The preference for Fletcher at that time is perhaps not hard to explain. He is remarkable for the easiness and agreeableness of his dialogue, which furthermore makes far less demand than Shakespeare's either upon the ability of the actor or the attention of the spectator. But the crowning reason for the preference then exhibited is something entirely different. Fletcher's comedies are upon a distinctly inferior plane of morality. The conversation is often coarse and at times actually offensive. The licentiousness characterizing it, which has largely contributed to drive these plays from the modern stage, undoubtedly added to their attraction at the period of the Restoration.[20]

The popularity of the Fletcherian romantic comedy and tragi-comedy is explainable upon the same grounds. Fletcher's romance is a step farther from life than Shakespeare's, an important item to an audience, which, priding itself upon its sophistication, would find more enjoyment in that which was obviously false, than in that which, while romantic, has a foundation of universal reality. Moreover, Fletcher's romantic comedies are distinguished by the same eroticism which marks his intrigue and manners comedies. It was this element which Restoration dramatists incorporated into their own tragi-comedies.

Very few, if any, elements in Restoration comedy can be definitely shown to be inheritances from Shakespeare. It has been suggested that the numerous romantic heroines—girls in male dress—might all have Viola of *Twelfth Night* as their common ancestor; but such characters were a common tradition of the stage. The average disguised heroine in comedy bears more resemblance to the Beaumont and Fletcher ladies in such plays as *The Night Walker*, while the heroine of

20 Lounsbury, T. R., *Shakespeare as a Dramatic Artist*, p. 266.

tragi-comedy bears more relation to the long suffering Euphrasia, of *Philaster*. Again, Colley Cibber might have been inspired to the central situation of *Love's Last Shift* by the example of *Measure for Measure*, but the treatment of the two situations is strikingly different. The typical cowards of the Restoration owe nothing to Falstaff, and the Portias are remarkable by their absence. The Restoration knew and cared too little about Shakespearean comedy to have been influenced by it.

CHAPTER III

ALTERATIONS, BORROWINGS AND IMITATIONS

Alterations

THE ATTITUDE of the Restoration toward Beaumont and Fletcher may be clearly shown by an examination of its alterations of plays by the older dramatists. Certainly there can be only two reasons why a Restoration dramatist should alter any of the older plays which were the stock property of the theatres. Either he had an honest desire to correct some actual fault, or something which his generation considered a fault, or else he wished to gain for himself fame and money by the reworking of a play which may have been popular once but was now forgotten. If we can find that the alterations of Beaumont and Fletcher plays are representative of Restoration tastes, we can see what relations are possible between the two groups of dramas. If, however, these alterations belong to the second type, those made wilfully for fame and money, they will tell us little.

Of the total of fifty-one plays[1] with which we are concerned here, the Restoration must have seen at least thirty-nine during the years 1660 to 1700. More it may have seen, for many of the plays which have left no record of production appear on the lists of old plays divided between the two companies after the return of Charles. Of these, twenty-seven were produced unaltered during the seventeenth century (four of them were later revised, early in the next century). Seven

[1] Omitting *The Widow*, by Jonson, Chapman and Fletcher, and *The Faithful Friends*, which was first printed from the original manuscript in 1812.

of the remaining twelve were altered after they had achieved some measure of popularity on the stage, and five were produced originally, (if our records may be trusted) in revised form. Of the twenty-seven unaltered plays it is certainly true that *The Beggars' Bush, The Humorous Lieutenant, A King and No King, The Maid's Tragedy, The Bloody Brother, Rule a Wife and Have a Wife, The Scornful Lady* and *Wit Without Money,* were decidedly popular. The other plays not altered were popular only in the first decade of the period. It is important to note that the Restoration did not confine its liking for the Beaumont and Fletcher plays to any one type—comedies of intrigue, manners and farce, tragi-comedies and tragedies are all represented.

We must consider then the alterations of sixteen plays; for, while four were altered in the eighteenth century, the alterations were made by dramatists who belong to both the Restoration and the period of so-called sentimentalism.[2] Of these, seven were alterations of comedies, seven of tragi-comedies, and two of tragedies. Their dates are important. Before 1670 only two, *The Two Noble Kinsmen* and *The Island Princess,* both tragi-comedies, were adapted. By 1680, two more, *Monsieur Thomas,* a comedy, and *The Pilgrim,* a tragi-comedy, had been added to the list. In the next decade five more were altered: *The Chances, The Noble Gentleman* and *The Sea Voyage,* comedies; *Valentinian,* a tragedy; and *The Prophetess,* a tragi-comedy. The three which were altered between 1690 and 1700 were *Bonduca,* a tragedy, and *Philaster,* and *A Wife for a Month,* tragi-comedies. Between 1700 and 1710 appeared alterations of *The Loyal Subject,* a

---

[2] I omit the alteration by Waller of *The Maid's Tragedy*. There is no evidence that this was ever performed.

tragi-comedy, and *Wit Without Money, Wit at Several Weapons* and *The Wild Goose Chase,* all comedies. Thus in the formative years of the Restoration, roughly 1660 to 1675, only four plays were altered, one of which was a comedy. As the century drew to its close the popularity of Beaumont and Fletcher waned, and the newer conceptions of sentimentalism and classicism in the eighteenth century brought about a constantly increasing number of alterations and revisions.

I shall summarize very briefly the important changes in each play.[3]

Tragedies

1. *Bonduca* altered to an opera by Powell, in 1696, does not seem to have appeared on the Restoration stage before that date. Originally a highly wrought, bombastic tragedy, it was made more sentimental and moral, considerably cut and generally mutilated to make it appropriate to the witless type of opera so popular with the Restoration.

2. *Valentinian* was altered by Rochester in 1684. The adapter seems to have had two main purposes in mind: to give the play unity of action, and to bring it more into the vein of heroic tragedy. In both he is successful, and his numerous minor changes seem to depend chiefly upon his main purposes. The result was a play, which it, must be admitted, is better than the original, a statement which can be made about very few Restoration adaptations of older dramas.

Tragi-comedy

1. *The Two Noble Kinsmen,* altered by Davenant and produced in 1664 under the name of *The Rivals,*

---

[3] For a complete analysis of each alteration see Sprague, A. C., *Beaumont and Fletcher on the Restoration Stage.* In general I have followed his conclusions, with some additions of my own.

seems on casual reading to be not altered at all. Yet we find on closer examination that the adapter has endeavoured to bring the play more in consonance with the neo-classic unities, to give a more careful motivation to the plot, and, perhaps unconsciously at this early date, to stress the "love and honor" motif, which is so important to the heroic play. These aims necessitated changes which are relatively slight.

2. *The Island Princess* went through three separate stages of alteration. The first revision, by an anonymous writer, appeared in 1669. It was "little more than Fletcher's melodrama abridged for acting purposes." [4] Such an abridgement need not concern us. The cutting was done, it seems, without consideration of what might best be spared.

The second alteration, by Tate in 1687, Professor Sprague suspects, reasonably enough, was based upon the earlier acting version. This, too, although now verging further upon complete alteration, bears the marks of an actable abridgement. For example we find[5] a brief dialogue between Panura, the princess' maid, and Quisana, the princess' aunt, who is elsewhere omitted. It is possible that Tate gave the printers the older version of the play, with his omissions and changes rather carelessly marked. The underplot is left out entirely and the heroic element is somewhat heightened. The characters have become amazingly moral.

The last version, by Motteux in 1689, is no longer Beaumont and Fletcher. The play has become an opera, with songs, masques, scenic devices and dramatic clap-trap of all kinds lugged in by the ears, while a tone of sentimental morality overspreads the whole.

---

[4] Sprague, op. cit. p. 137.
[5] Act IV, 2.

3. *The Prophetess* was altered by Betterton in 1690 to an opera, with the addition of music and the enhancing of spectacular scenes. Usually when a good play was transformed into an opera the result was deplorable to say the least. *The Prophetess*, however, was so near the operatic form in its original condition that few changes were needed.

4. Vanbrugh's alteration of *The Pilgrim*, in 1670, shows very few changes and none of importance. The fine poetry of the original is paraphrased and cut, and much unnecessary detail is omitted.

5. *Philaster* was "improved upon" by the conscientious and moral Elkanah Settle. After 1695 it was seen upon the stage under its own name, but with his alterations. It seems to have been very popular before it was tampered with. The important alterations are two: the softening of the scene between Philaster, Arethusa and Bellario, in response to a popular (or perhaps rather critical) feeling that it was indecorous for a lover to wound his mistress,[6] and the heightening of the character of Philaster to bring the play more in accord with the heroic tradition. The sentimental and moral notes are struck with a vigorous hand.[7]

6. *A Wife for a Month*, Fletcher's extremely theatrical and somewhat meretricious tragi-comedy, was made into a tragedy in 1697 by Scott. It was renamed *The Unhappy Kindness*. Neo-classicism played a fairly important part in the alteration, which, in fact, is probably a better play than the original, because of its compactness. The main outlines of plot and character are retained.

7. *The Faithful General*, by M. N., was produced in 1705. It is a highly sentimentalized corruption of *The*

[6] See Dryden, *The Defense of the Epilogue*, Scott-Saintsbury, IV, pp. 229-30.

[7] Professor Sprague analyses another alteration of Philaster (op. cit. p. 187) which was never produced.

Loyal Subject. The classic unities play some part in the motive of the work, but on the whole it defies analysis. It is diffuse, lengthy, stilted and tedious.[8]

Comedy

1. *The Chances* was improved by the Duke of Buckingham in 1682. This is one of the rare examples of an alteration which is better than the original. That Fletcher's comedy needed improvement is obvious. The first three acts are excellent, but from then on the dramatist flagged. Villiers left the first three acts practically intact, but rewrote the last two entirely. The play was popular both before and after its alteration.

2. *Monsieur Thomas*, after years of obscurity, fell into the merciless hands of D'Urfey and suffered. The new play, under the title of *Trick for Trick or the Debauch'd Hypocrite*, appeared in 1678. The romantic subplot of the original is practically lost, and the comic characters are coarsened until they are almost unrecognizable. "The Thomas of *Trick for Trick* is no longer an amusingly mischievous rattlepate, but a filthy 'debauched hypocrite.' In short, D'Urfey has vulgarized Fletcher's rather risque but amusing comedy." [9] The plot is much changed, but the language of Fletcher is often retained, especially where wit is most desired.

[8] See Genest, II, p. 346. "In the preface to *The Loyal Subject*, as reprinted in 1706, it is said that the original play had been well received on its revival—and that when the legitimate offspring of Fletcher appeared on the stage the very same day as the By-blow did, the town quitted the impostor to embrace the legitimate."

[9] Forsythe, R. S. *A Study of the Plays of Thomas D'Urfey*, p. 23. The prologue to this play contains a statement typical of adapters:

"On the foundation Fletcher laid, he built;
New dressed his modish spark fit to be shown,
And made him more debauched to oblige the town.
Drink, rant and sing, he now takes pains to be
A perfect and accomplished Debauchee."

3. *The Sea Voyage* appeared in 1685 under the guise of *A Commonwealth of Women*. D'Urfey made fewer changes in this. In general, as in his other alterations of Beaumont and Fletcher plays, he has debased the characters and coarsened the language. The original, one would think, was sufficiently indecent; but its indecency was of the subtle type more peculiar to the Restoration. D'Urfey substituted obscenity for indecency. The plot is somewhat changed, for no particular reason. The first act, almost entirely D'Urfey's, requires following changes.

4. *The Noble Gentleman* was a not particularly remarkable farce-comedy to begin with, but D'Urfey's alteration of it, in 1688, under the name of *A Fool's Preferment or the Three Dukes of Dunstable*, is decidedly remarkable and more farcical. Some satire on contemporary matters, notably the playing of basset, is introduced; one entire sub-plot is omitted, and another, more farcical, is developed more fully. The exaggeration of farce at the conclusion is beyond all bounds of probability. And, of course, we notice the same coarsening of characters and broadening of wit which distinguishes all of D'Urfey's work. There seems to have been no reason for altering the plays, except that none of them was on the stage at the time.

5. Farquhar's alteration of *The Wild Goose Chase* as *The Inconstant*, 1702, represents little more than the bringing to light of a forgotten play.[10] One or two characters are combined; the verse is consistently turned into prose, and a new, somewhat bawdy scene is added in the fifth act. The chief character, Mirabel,

[10] In his preface Farquhar says: "I shall only say that I took the hint from Fletcher's *Wild Goose Chase*; and to those who say I have spoiled the original, I wish no other injury but that they say it again."

now Bob Mirabel, is the same as before," and his mistress, Oriana, has only one new duty, that of acting the romantic part of a girl in boy's clothing. The minor omissions and additions seem to be the result of caprice only. The play, as the dramatist admits in his preface, was not a success—why, it is difficult to say, unless, as he suggests, the attractions of foreign entertainers at the other house were too strong.

6. An anonymous acting version of *Wit Without Money,* previously a popular play, appeared in 1707. It contained only slight changes in dialogue. By this date, of course, many words and phrases had become antequated. A general softening of the bawdy language is noticed.

7. *Wit at Several Weapons,* rarely, if ever, produced during the Restoration, was altered by Colley Cibber in 1709 and appeared on the stage under the name of *The Rival Fools.* In spite of Cibber's prologue [12] there are surprisingly few changes of importance, even the names suggesting those of the original characters. The verse is consistently turned to prose, most of it a close paraphrase of the original. Obscenity and wit are neither lessened nor enhanced. Cibber has somewhat improved the action in the closing scenes.

Love Makes a Man and *The City Ramble*

There remain two more comedies in the Restoration tradition, not considered by Professor Sprague, which,

[11] In the words of the epilogue:
> "A witty wild, inconstant, free gallant,
> With a gay soul, with sense and will to rove,
> With language and with softness framed to move,
> With little truth but with a world of love."

[12] "From Sprightly Fletcher's loose confed'rate muse
> The unfinish'd hints of these light scenes we choose,
> For with such careless haste this play was writ,
> So unperus'd each thought of started wit;
> Each weapon of his wit so lamely fought,
> That 'twould as scanty on our stage be thought,
> As for a modern belle my granum's petticoat."

while not exactly alterations of Beaumont and Fletcher plays, are still something more than examples of borrowing. These are Cibber's *Love Makes a Man*, produced in 1701, and *The City Ramble; or The Playhouse Wedding*, by Elkanah Settle, 1711. They belong to that type of adaptation which is perhaps best illustrated by Davenant's well known combination of *Measure for Measure* with the Benedick-Beatrice sub-plot from *Much Ado About Nothing* to make the new play called *The Law Against Lovers*.

1. *Love Makes a Man* is composed of patches from two of Beaumont and Fletcher's plays: *The Elder Brother and The Custom of the Country*. In the main it is a skillful piece of work, joining as it does two plots, which, however, have characters with much in common. Beaumont and Fletcher made use of rather stereotyped characters, who are repeated over and over in different comedies.

Act I of Cibber's play is a free rendition of Act I, 2, and Act II, 1, of *The Elder Brother*. Some necessary additions of exposition give the act continuity. Act II is an almost literal paraphrase of II, 2, of *The Elder Brother*. Here occurs the break between the plot of *The Elder Brother* and that of *The Custom of the Country*. In the first play the lovers are driven from home; in Cibber's version they run away and take ship as in Act I of *The Custom of the Country*. Now the plot of the second play comes into action.

Act III is taken almost verbatim from Act II of *The Custom of the Country*. The character of Don Lewis, a lewd old blusterer, is carried over from *The Elder Brother,* and the part of Rutilio, in *The Custom of the Country* is filled by Clodio, the gay young gallant of the first play. In the last two acts Cibber varies rather widely from his models. Act IV is drawn chiefly from

Act II, 2 and Act IV, 1 and 3, of *The Custom of the Country*. Changes in the last acts were necessary, of course, because of the combination of the two plots. Even so, Cibber has managed to tack on an ending to his olla podrida which is not too far from that of the original play.

Surprisingly enough the result is a good lively comedy. There is little in it which is really Cibber's. His skill as a dramatist comes in play chiefly in his ability to select and arrange. He has taken the wittiest, cleverest, most luscious parts of the two comedies. One scene he must have omitted with reluctance:—that in which Rutilio is hired by the bawd, Sulpitia, for the accommodation of certain ladies of quality. This would have probably proved too strong for the nice refinement of the end of the century. On the same grounds, perhaps, he has softened Fletcher's frank exposition of the situation in which Duarte believes that his mother is in love with his supposed murderer. But, on the other hand, the very colorful tempting of Arnaldo by Hippolita is not only retained but amplified. The distinction, of course, is between frankness and suggestiveness.

Other changes are those suggested by the exigencies of this type of work. Cibber's change of Duomar, Duarte's mother, into Elvira, his sister, is certainly dramatically better and more plausible. The character of Eustace, in *The Elder Brother*, renamed Clodio, is modernized into a more typical wild gallant. He now has all the characteristics of Eustace, plus those of the lecherous, roaring, swearing, Rutilio.

The best of the play, verbally, is that paraphrased from Fletcher. Where it has been necessary to connect the different sections with new dialogue, the difference between Cibber's language and his paraphrase of

Fletcher is striking. Perhaps he realized his own deficiencies, in comparison to the older poet, for, in the conclusion to the play, a very effective scene, he has copied Fletcher direct. No credit was given to the older dramatist in either prologue or epilogue.

2. *The City Ramble or the Playhouse Wedding* is based on *The Knight of the Burning Pestle* and *The Coxcomb*. Although no credit for the borrowings was given in either prologue or epilogue, when the play was printed Settle acknowledged his debt in the preface and, amazingly enough, surrounded with quotation marks the lines purloined from the older plays. Although he claimed to have used his sources only as foundation, we find that in reality he made a rather ingenious collation of selections, with the addition of one important situation of his own invention. The opening lines of Act I, 1 and Act II, 1, some thirteen lines in Act II, 3, and almost all of Act II, 5 and 6, Act III, 1 and 3, Act IV, 1, and the latter part of Act V, 1, are nearly verbatim selections from the two older plays, chiefly *The Coxcomb*. Settle blended together, not unskillfully, the plot dealing with the scorned apprentice and the master's daughter, from *The Knight of the Burning Pestle*, and the Ricardo-Viola sub-plot, from *The Coxcomb*. The "frame" used in *The Knight of the Burning Pestle*,—i.e. the citizens on the stage, who interpolate comments—is made use of, with the transformation of the old merchant, his wife, and the apprentice, into a city councilman, his wife and their daughter. The connection of the daughter with one of the players gives the excuse for the secondary title.

The characters show relatively few changes. The Count, descendant of Humphrey in *The Knight of the Burning Pestle*, is a somewhat heightened and embellished character. He is placed in a new and farcical situation, designed to bring him in bad odor with the master. Viola, originally a sentimental heroine, is made more so, and Ricardo's penitence for his cavalier mistreatment of her reaches the heights of rant. The Chevalier Garcia, who falls in love with Viola, does not disappear from the story, as does Valerio, his original, but, after philanthropically giving away all his wealth, hies him to a monastery to heal his broken heart.

The only other important change is in the diction, a mixture of blank verse and prose, which, where it is Settle's, is highly sentimental, and where it is Fletcher's, is made more abstract. In place of Fletcher's Anglo-Saxon strength, we have discreet paraphrases.

It is noticeable that of the four plays used as foundation material for these two adaptations, none had been at all popular in the Restoration, yet they were chosen for use by two men who were, if not inspired, at least successful playwrights.

Typical Changes

Professor Sprague has listed a number of typical changes made in these plays, in an attempt to classify them.[13] It is not my intention to take up each minor point and discuss it separately; many of his classifications are based upon an insufficient number of examples to permit generalization. I wish rather to point out what happened in the main to Beaumont and Fletcher's plays, when they fell into the hands of adapters. We may say, for example, of Shakespeare, that the Restoration objected to his "obsolete and coarse" diction, and so rewrote it; that the heroes of his tragedies were not exaggerated enough, hence they exaggerated them; that his wit was not witty enough,

[13] Op. cit., p. 263.

not obscene enough, and so on—and any number of alterations bear out these conclusions.

On the other hand, the following statements may be said to hold with the alterations of Beaumont and Fletcher plays:

1. We cannot generalize from the example of only two tragedies, *Bonduca* and *Valentinian*, which were altered for entirely different reasons and in different directions.

2. Tragi-comedies were changed in line with the following ideas.

A. That the rules of neo-classic decorum should be more strictly observed.

B. That morality and sentiment should play an even greater part than in the originals. Especially is this true in those alterations which were made toward the close of the century.

C. That the heroic elements, in character, setting and plot, should be more emphasized.[14]

Yet, although we find all of these ideas at work to some degree in all the alterations of tragi-comedies, it is questionable whether they represent all or only a part of Restoration sentiment. While *The Two Noble Kinsmen*, to use one example, was affected by the rules of neo-classicism, at the same time half a dozen plays by Beaumont and Fletcher, which paid little heed to the unities, were deservedly popular. While *The Island Princess* was altered in such a way as to avoid the mixture of the romantic and the comic, on the other hand, such plays were being produced by Restoration dramatists. Dryden, alone, has five such to his credit. And as for morality and sentiment,—it would be strange, indeed, if the time of Charles the Second were

[14] For a thorough study of this, see Tupper, J. W., *The Relation of the Heroic Play to Beaumont and Fletcher*, P. M. L. A., XX.

more moral than that of his father. This tendency, rather, is an indication of two things: the strain of rant which reached its climax in the heroic play, and the rising tide of bourgeois morality which resulted in Collier's attack on the stage and the slow reformation of the drama. But the sentimental and moral element is later than the heroic, which, however, seems to be typical of all Restoration tragi-comedy. We have the peculiar situation of the Beaumont and Fletcher tragi-comedy giving birth to the heroic play, and, when its child has grown to maturity, being remodeled to suit the latter's changed ideals!

3 When we consider the alterations of comedies, we find that we can generalize only to the extent of saying that the verse of Beaumont and Fletcher was nearly always reduced to prose. The fact that D'Urfey made three comedies into vulgar farces is an indication, not of the fact that the Restoration preferred vulgar farce, but that D'Urfey did, and with him, of course, a certain element of the audiences. On the other hand, we have three alterations, those of *Wit at Several Weapons, Wit Without Money,* and *The Wild Goose Chase,* in which no important changes of character or tone were made. And against the "combination" play of Settle, with its heightening of morality and heart interest, we may set the similar work of Cibber, which, while softening the Jacobean coarseness of its sources, heightened their more subtle obscenity. Only one alteration, that of *The Chances,* is indicative of a feeling that the play was faulty, and here the fault was one of construction, from which we cannot generalize.

Eleven comedies by Beaumont and Fletcher formed the basis for nine Restoration comedies. The statements of the adapters, or their lack of statements, clearly show that they hoped the audiences would not realize how closely the originals had been followed. Of these eleven comedies, only one, *The Chances*, had been really popular on the stage before its alteration. The others either had never been produced, or had been forgotten. Clearly then, these alterations represent the deliberate rifling of the storehouses of the past, and the changing of the purloined riches beyond recognition, in order to give credit (and money) to the astute thieves. There is nothing about them which leads us to believe that the adapters were inspired by an earnest and reverent desire to bring good old plays up to date.[15]

It is easy to see why more plays were not so altered. The Restoration burglars chose very well; if we look from the Restoration point of view at the plays which were not altered and were not popular in their original form, we find that the remaining twelve were rather a poor lot. Why these altered plays were not popular in their original form, it is less easy to see. Some of them were, of course, in the first decade of the period. *The Wild Goose Chase*, "that famous play" as Pepys called it,[16] may be taken as an example. There is enough evidence to show that it must have been popular in the first years of the Restoration, yet, so far as our fragmentary records show, it dropped out of sight until its alteration in 1702. In almost every respect

[15] We may quote here Lacy, contemporary actor and playwright, who was well qualified to discuss his fellow dramatists.

Sir Hercules. Ay, and some of 'em will filch and steal out o' th' old plays, and cry down the authors when they've done.

Squire Buffoon. They have no more invention than there is in the head of a soused mackerel. Now they've turned cobblers; they vamp and mend old plays.

Sir Hercules. Or rather turned tinkers, who stop one holde and make ten; so they mend one fault and make twenty. *Sir Hercules Buffoon, Act II, iv.*

[16] Diary, January 11, 1668.

this is a typical Restoration comedy, with wit, intrigue, obscenity, satire of manners, and wild, sophisticated couples; and when Farquhar altered it he had very little to do. But there are many possible reasons for its disappearance, in the chaotic and uneven course of the late seventeenth century stage, which have nothing to do with its agreement or non-agreement with Restoration tastes.

Our result, then, in the consideration of the alterations of comedies, is largely negative. If these alterations do not represent the general trend of Restoration practise, they cannot tell us that the Restoration was dissatisfied with the Beaumont and Fletcher types of comedies. It must be true, then, that, since the Restoration, that period from 1660 to 1700, saw and liked twenty-seven plays of Beaumont and Fletcher in unaltered form (twelve of them comedies or tragi-comedies in which the comic portion is of greatest importance and scope) that it saw, and presumably liked, twelve more in altered form, of which four were comedies; that three more of the first group of comedies were only slightly altered in the early eighteenth century, and two "combination" plays, based on four of the comedies popular earlier were produced in the same first decade of the next century—therefore there must have been very close agreements between the Beaumont and Fletcher and the Restoration types of comedies, with corresponding reason for believing in the influence of the former upon the latter.

The use by the Restoration dramatists of Beaumont and Fletcher's plays as a sort of quarry from which to hew out new comedies, is one proof that the later playwrights held their masters in respect, as writers of full bodied, well developed dramatic entertainments.

Another sort of proof is added by an inspection of the
Restoration borrowings from and imitations of the
works of the two Jacobeans. I shall consider here first
only the more definite borrowings, i.e. those which are
proved by parallel passages, or in which the congruent
elements are unmistakably parallel.[17] By borrowings I
mean: direct plagiarism of dialogues, plots, characters
or situations, further elaborated, usually, by the Restoration dramatist. In doubtful cases I have gone on
the principle that the dramatist would be more likely
to go to the Beaumont and Fletcher source, a play
which was probably on the stage at the time of the
plagiarism, or earlier, rather than to some obscure
novel, perhaps in a foreign tongue.

Borrowings

1. That indefatigable hunter out of plagiarists,
Langbaine, has pointed out in discussing John Corye's
The Generous Enemies or the Ridiculous Lovers, that
"The quarrel between Bertran and Robatzy in the fifth
act is stolen verbatim from *Love's Pilgrimage* [by
Beaumont and Fletcher] Act II, 2, and II, 3."[18] This
is certainly true, but Langbaine has missed other borrowings from the same play. In fact, Corye's romantic
comedy bears a striking likeness in general to the
older play.

A sample of one of the plagiarisms Langbaine missed

[17] It is possible, of course, to pile up any number of examples of rather
doubtful authenticity. Such a questionable borrowing would be that suggested by Genest (II, p. 549) that the manorial custom situation, in Charles
Johnson's *The Country Lasses* (1715,) is suggested by Fletcher's *The Custom
of the Country,* a statement which Mr. Nicoll accepts without question in his
History of Eighteenth Century Drama. Yet this minor situation, a farcical
handling of the "droit du seigneur," which is given a tragic implication in
Fletcher's play, bears not the slightest resemblance to the older drama.

[18] *Account of the English Dramatic Poets,* p. 73.

may be quoted. In Corye's play appeared the following passage: [19]

(Enter Jacintha and Livia Veyld)

ALVARO.   Hold, yonder's a lady veyld,
    For shape and motion much resembling Alleria.
LYSANDER.   Dear sir, forbear, I must not suffer you;
    Do you not know the custom of the place?
    To draw the curtain in the street (though she were
    mean) is mortal.

From *Love's Pilgrimage* we have the following: [20]

(Enter Eugenia with Divers attendants)

MARC-ANTONIO.   'Slight, sir! yonder is a lady veil'd;
    For properness beyond comparison,
    And sure her face is like the rest; we'll see't.
GENTLEMAN.   Why, you are hasty, sir, already. Know you
    What 'tis you go about?
MARC-ANTONIO.   Yes; I would see
    The woman's face.
GENTLEMAN.   By Heaven you shall not do't!
    You do not know the custom of the place;
    To draw that curtain here, though she were mean,
    Is mortal.

Why this particular theft should have taken place
it is difficult to see, unless we accept the theory that
Corye was seeking for bright bits with which to polish
up a rather dull play. The situation introduced ends
only in anti-climax, when Alvaro discovers that the
veiled lady is his sister.

The plot and characters of the play are clearly based
on those of *Love's Pilgrimage*. Both are romantic
comedies, dealing with cross-purpose love affairs. In
Love's Pilgrimage we have two ladies, who had been
promised marriage by the same man, following their
common lover in mannish disguises. Cory has reduced the number of disguised ladies to one, but he has

[19] *The Generous Enemies*, Act. IV, 1.
[20] *Love's Pilgrimage*, Act IV; 1.

two other love-lorn damsels, not disguised, in pursuit of a would-be bigamous lover, Cassidoro, who finds himself in a situation much resembling that of Marc-Antonio in the older play. The confusion of plot is hopeless. Important here is the use of the romantic device first employed by Beaumont and Fletcher—the mating of a rejected lover or mistress to a man or woman who has previously shown no affection for the jilted one. This is a much used device in Restoration comedy. It is always a perfectly heartless mating, based upon that philosophy in which Beaumont and Fletcher were at one with the Restoration, that love was a transient thing, to be employed for amusement only, and marriage, consequently, a matter of convenience. In *Love's Pilgrimage*, Leocadia, rejected at last by Marc-Antonio, is easily persuaded to marry Phillipo.[21] In *The Generous Enemies*, Jacintha, who has been jilted by Cassidoro, is consoled by Flamino, who has shown little affection for her up to this time.

2. In D'Urfey's *The Campaigners*, (1698) a situation arises in which Colonel Dorange, the hero, unwittingly becomes the custodian of a bundle of infant's attire. The scene in which he is depicted as receiving the bundle is strikingly similar to that in Beaumont and Fletcher's *The Chances*, in which Don John receives a bundle containing an infant. I quote first from *The Campaigners*.[22]

GUSSETT. Hist, hist, are you there?
DORANGE. Hah—what's that, a woman's voice?
GUSSET. Are you there, I say?
DORANGE. Aye, aye.
GUESSET. Come underneath then and catch and stay below till we come down. (Throws down bundle and exit)

---

[21] This is much more logically developed in the source for the play: Cervantes, *Exemplary Novels, The Two Damsels.*
[22] *The Campaigners*, Act I, 2.

DORANGE. So, I have got it, but what I have catched, or who the
devil they take me for, I can't so much as guess—hum—
'tis a bundle, and if I feel right—silk and laced—oh—
for a rich purchase of shining pearl or glittering dia-
monds, now, which some pretty young wanton has
packed together to run away with from her lover, from
some damnable cross old aunt, or confounded mother-
in-law, whilst I, guided by my propitious stars, in spite
of darkness am ordained to be the lucky supplanter.

And from *The Chances.*[23]

WOMAN (*within*) Signior?
DON JOHN. What? How is this?
WOMAN (*within*) Signior Fabricio?
DON JOHN. I'll go nearer.
WOMAN (*within*) Fabricio?
DON JOHN. This is a woman's tongue; here may be good done.
WOMAN (*within*) Who's there? Fabricio?
DON JOHN. Aye.
WOMAN (*within*) Where are you?
DON JOHN. Here.
WOMAN (*within*) Oh, come, for Heaven's sake!
DON JOHN. I must see what this means.
            (*Enter woman with bundle from house*)
WOMAN. I have staid this long hour for you. Make no noise.
For things are in a strange trouble. Here, be secret;
'tis worth your care. Begone now; more eyes watch us
than may be for our safeties.
DON JOHN. Hark you!
WOMAN. Peace! Good night!
DON JOHN. She is gone and I am loaden; Fortune for me! It
weighs well and it feels well; it may chance to be some
pack of worth: by the mass, 'tis heavy! If it be coin
or jewels, 'tis worth welcome; I'll ne'er refuse a fortune. I am confident 'tis of no common price. Now to
my lodging! If it hit right, I'll bless this night.

This parallelism, when taken into consideration with
the fact that the central situation of both comedies has
to do with an illegitimate child, whose mother is later
married to the hero, or another, minor character would

[23] *The Chances*, Act I, 3.

seem to indicate that D'Urfey had *The Chances* in mind while he was writing his play.

3. Genest remarks of Dryden's romantic comedy, *The Rival Ladies,* that "there is some resemblance between this play and *Love's Pilgrimage."*[24] The resemblance, however, is of such a type that were it not for one element it would be as easy to believe that Dryden went direct to Fletcher's source, or to some other novel or novels.[25] But one important addition made by Fletcher to Cervantes' plot was that of another woman character with whom Marc-Antonio, the hero, already in love with two women to whom he had promised marriage, might further complicate the action. This addition Dryden has taken and still further enlarged upon, turning a light, romantic comedy into something nearer tragi-comedy. Although he has added new scenes and incidents in the heroic manner, the general parallelism of plot, and the one clear example of a character found only in the two plays and not in the sources, show that there was a definite relationship between the two.

4. Further evidence of Dryden's general indebtedness to Beaumont and Fletcher has already been pointed out in connection with *The Spanish Friar.*[26] Here again we have the question whether Dryden went to the Beaumont and Fletcher comedy, *The Spanish Curate,* or to the source for the older play, *Gerardo, the Unfortunate Spaniard,* a novel by Goncal de Cespedes, a translation of which appeared in 1622.[27] Beaumont and Fletcher developed the romantic characters of the novel, Leandro and Violante, into Leandro,

[24] Genest, op. cit., I, p. 50.

[25] Cf. for suggested sources, *Biographia Dramatica,* II, 309.

[26] Saintsbury, Mermaid Series, *Dryden,* II, 112.

[27] For the full title and that portion of the romance which forms the basis of *The Spanish Curate,* see Dyce, Works of B&F, VIII, 373-392.

a very wild gallant, and Amaranta, a clever, unscrupulous wife. The lawyer Bartolus, Amaranta's husband, is merely a jealous lawyer in the romance; in the comedy he is also crusty, miserly, suspicious, and generally villainous. The vicar of the romance is a most shadowy character; his cupidity is stressed, but after his first duty of introducing Leandro to Bartolus' house, he practically disappears. In *The Spanish Curate* he is given a much larger part. He is represented as constantly at swords points with Bartolus, as taking part in schemes which are not merely below his priestly functions, but decidedly rascally, and at the end is within an ace of being turned out of his living.

Dryden took the same group of characters from Fletcher and carried them still further in the directions indicated in the older play. His Lorenzo is more cynical, more open in his lasciviousness than Leandro; his Elvira is of a lower, more hoydenish type than Amaranta; his Bartolus is more disgusting. Dominic, the friar, is now a long way from the faint figure of romance. Like his prototype in *The Spanish Curate* he is a rascal; but now he is also a pander—he is more nauseous than amusing. Yet it is upon his character, mainly, that we must build our proof that Dryden went to the Beaumont and Fletcher comedy rather than to the novel, since he, of all the dramatis personae, is almost no character in the romance, but much the same individual in the two plays.

Another theme in *The Spanish Friar* may serve to connect that comedy with another Beaumont and Fletcher play, *Women Pleased*. The theme of both the Beaumont and Fletcher plays, like that of Dryden, is the attempt of a lover to get access to his mistress, whose husband has the knack of appearing at inopportune moments. The situations in the three plays are

alike in principle, but they differ in application sufficiently to show that Dryden took from *The Spanish
Curate* only the theme and the characters. From the
sub-plot of *Women Pleased* he may have taken the
subtle suggestion of incest. At the conclusion of
Women Pleased we learn that the lover, Claudio, is the
brother of his would-be mistress, Isabella, and has
only been trying her virtue. At the close of *The Spanish Friar*, Lorenzo and Elvira learn, to their surprise,
that they are brother and sister. There is nothing,
however, in the earlier acts of either play, to suggest
to us that the two ladies are at all backward or modest
in their love making. The situations, of course, are
exceedingly spicy.[28]

5. As Montague Summers has pointed out, in
speaking of Congreve's *The Double Dealer*: "There is
a close resemblance, too close to be accidental, between the dialogue when Lady Touchwood arouses her
husband by subtle lying hints[29] and Fletcher's scene in
Cupid's Revenge[30] where Bacha cunningly inflames the
old duke against his son Leucippus.[31] But this is not
all; the character of Maskwell, in Congreve's play, is
largely founded upon that of Timanthus, in *Cupid's
Revenge*, and Mellefont, the hero of the Restoration
comedy, is closely related to Leucippus.[32] Lady Touchwood suggests, rather than resembles Bacha.

The plot of *Cupid's Revenge* is taken from a brief

[28] There is the further possibility that Dryden may have been influenced
here by the success of Beaumont and Fletcher's *A King and No King*, on
the Restoration stage. This play, dealing as it does with the question of
incest in a more serious way, yet not tragically, has been suggested as a
source for Dryden's *Love Triumphant*. As a source it is doubtful, but it may
have furnished inspiration.

[29] *The Double Dealer*, III, 1.

[30] *Cupid's Revenge*, IV, 2.

[31] *Works of Congreve*, II, p. 3.

[32] Davies first pointed out: "Maskwell's character is partly taken
. . . I think, from the Timanthus of Fletcher's *Cupid's Revenge*." *Dramatic
Miscellanies* III, 320.

passage in Sidney's *Arcadia*, Book II, which, while containing the outline, only slightly develops the characters. The particular situation which Congreve borrowed from Fletcher, is a version of the Potiphar's wife story. As Fletcher gives it, Bacha, formerly Leucippus' mistress, now his step-mother, tempts him, and is scorned. In revenge she insinuates to her husband that her honor has been attacked. Aided by Timanthus, who pretends friendship to Leucippus, she succeeds in convincing her husband, who orders his son arrested. Congreve's version is essentially the same, but more seriously treated. Mellefont, as nice in his honor as Leucippus, is loved by his aunt, Lady Touchwood, whose honor is not proof against her lust. Maskwell, Mellefont's false friend, secret lover of Lady Touchwood, and generally an accomplished villain, aids his mistress to persuade Lord Touchwood that his nephew has designs upon her honor.

A further parallel may be drawn between Careless, who consistently warns Mellefont against Maskwell, to be as often laughed at for his pains, and Ismenus, the cousin of Leucippus, who plays the same role in the older play. This character is not found in the novel.

That Congreve borrowed his plot from Fletcher and not from Sidney, is clearly shown by the fact that, while the situations in the two plays are developed fully along very similar lines, Sidney dismissed the whole matter in a very few sentences.

6. The underplot of Hopkins' *Neglected Virtue,* is an unmistakable borrowing from Beaumont and Fletcher's *The Pilgrim.* In Hopkins' comedy, Amadine's father, Bretton, insists on her marrying a fop, Cachlio, as in the older play Alinda's father insists that she marry an outlaw, Roderigo. Each girl runs away, aided in one case by a sharp tongued maid, in the other by an

equally sharp tongued cousin. Both girls take refuge
in boy's attire, pretend madness to escape their respective fathers, and by similar tricks succeed in having their parents confined in madhouses while they are
marrying their lovers. Hopkins has done a poor piece
of patchwork, his stolen material blending hardly at
all with the main portion of his plot.

7. It is always difficult to trace the borrowing of
characters, yet one example of this sort of theft is
very clear, and is important as showing that Shadwell
was under the influences of Beaumont and Fletcher
as well as of Jonson. In the *Volunteers* or *The Stock-
jobbers*, (1693) occurs the character of Sir Timothy
Kastril, a minor bully. Kastril's name is taken probably from Kastril, the "angry boy" in *The Alchemist*.
He is an unquestioned "humors" character, yet his
characteristics are those, not of his namesake, but of
La-writ, in Beaumont and Fletcher's *The Little French
Lawyer*. Like his model, Sir Timothy is a cowardly fellow, who has been in the habit of accepting insults and
blows with equal meekness. Again like his model, he is
fairly forced into a duel, and meeting with one more
cowardly than himself, wins. Thenceforth, like
La-writ, Sir Timothy roars and bullies, picking quar-
rels on the slightest provocation. The speeches of the
two characters are alike in content but not in form.

This particular borrowing suggests that perhaps the
influence of Beaumont and Fletcher should be seen as
applied also in the field of "humors" characterization.
Undoubtedly they made use of Jonson's method, more,
however, for its dramatic effectiveness than its moral
value. They may have formed one of the inter-
mediaries to which, I suspect, Restoration dramatists
went for their models of character development, as
much as to Jonson himself.

Imitations

These few examples of borrowings serve to indicate definitely the relationship between the Jacobean and the Restoration dramatists. Further evidence of much the same sort of connection is furnished by an examination of some of the more decided Restoration imitations of situations developed in the Beaumont and Fletcher comedies. These I call imitations, rather than borrowings, because there cannot be definite proof of a relationship. We are justified, however, in assuming an imitation, first, when the parallelism between the two situations is reasonably clear; second, when the situations are rather unusual, that is, not the stock material of both the old and the newer drama; and third, because the logical assumption always to be made is that the imitator would be following that which he had seen acclaimed on the contemporary stage. The danger in dealing with such imitations is that one is tempted to say that such and such a situation, idea or character "suggests" a similar dramatic device in one of Beaumont and Fletcher's plays. I shall restrict myself, therefore, to an examination of only the more obvious and reasonable imitations.

1. Much of the romantic plot in James Howard's *All Mistaken, or the Mad Couple*, (1667) is in imitation of Beaumont and Fletchers' *A King and No King*. Briefly the plot of the older play is as follows: King Arbaces, returning from war, brings with him his prisoner, Tigranes, to whom he has promised his sister, Panthea, as wife. Arbaces, seeing his sister for the first time in years, falls in love with her, becomes jealous of Tigranes, whom he imprisons, and locks up Panthea, partly to keep her away from himself, and partly to keep her from visiting Tigranes. After a succession of

sensuous and violent scenes, Arbaces discovers that Panthea is not his sister and so is free to marry him. Spaconia, Tigranes' true love in his own country, who has visited him and scolded him in prison, is at last married to her lover.

The Restoration tragi-comedy seems to have used an inversion of this plot. The Duke returns from war, accompanied by his captive, Zoranzo, and by Artabella, whom he plans to marry. He really loves Amphelia, who returns his love, but each holds to a belief that he is scorned by the other. Zoranzo is imprisoned and later is visited by Amphelia, from motives of pity only. The Duke, becoming insanely jealous, orders them confined together in chains, and later beheaded. While they are in prison they are visited by Amarissa, Zoranzo's true love in his own country. Her tirade smacks strongly of that of Spaconia, in the older play. The mistake of Amphelia and the Duke is dramatically cleared up on the scaffold, and the question of what he shall do with Artabella is neatly solved when the latter is found to be the Duke's long lost sister. Zoranzo and Amarissa are united.

The similarity of the two plots is obvious. Of course Howard might have gone to the novel, or what ever it was, which Beaumont and Fletcher used as a foundation for their play, but no source for *A King and No King* has been discovered. The work of the Restoration dramatist bears all the earmarks of an imitation done by a man who wished to make use of what he saw was a good situation, yet who wished to cover up his tracks at the same time. The play is hastily written, immature, and poorly motivated.

2. In Beaumont and Fletcher's *The Custom of the Country* Arnoldo is led by a servant of Hyppolita to the latter's house, where he finds a rich feast spread for

him.[33]   Here, amid the most sensuous surroundings, he
is entertained by Hyppolita, who tempts him with
every trick of the stage vampire. The suggestiveness
of the whole scene is the sort of thing that must have
appealed strongly to the Restoration.

As I have noted before, when Colley Cibber used
this play he retained the temptation scene nearly intact. His hero, however, is not lured to the home of
Louisa, but is kidnaped by her servants. This change
may have been suggested to Cibber by the similar scene
in Otway's *The Atheist* (1683) with which we are concerned here as an imitation. In Otway's comedy [34]
Beaugarde, who loves Porcia, a rich young widow, is
abducted by her masked servants and brought to her
house. Here is spread the rich feast; the surroundings
are as voluptuous as possible, and Porcia, masqued,
makes love to Beaugarde. The development of the
story, however, is changed by the arrival of other characters, who turn the plot into farcical channels. Significantly there are no organic purposes in introducing
the situation; it does not only fail to advance the action
— it is a positive hindrance to the dramatic unity of the
plot. Obviously it was lugged in bodily as a nice titil-
lation to the senses of the Restoration audience.

3. In another of Otway's comedies, *The Soldier's
Fortune*, (1680) Langbaine professed to find a strong
likeness to a situation in Beaumont and Fletcher's
Monsieur Thomas. In the latter play the scene is as
follows: Thomas, attempting to get access to Mary,
his scornful mistress, serenades her. She appears at
an upper window. Thomas, in trying to scale the wall,
falls to the ground and pretends to have broken his
leg, a device which deceives Mary temporarily. When

[33] *The Custom of the Country*, II, 1.
[34] *The Atheist*, III, 2.

Thomas rises to his feet, after she has come to the rescue, she tricks him, and locks him out.[35]

In *The Soldier's Fortune* we have parallel characters in the wild soldier, Courtine, and his disdainful mistress, Sylvia. The scene which Langbaine refers to is, however, not a clear parallel.[36] Courtine attempts to get to Sylvia's balcony on a rope. He is pulled half way up, and left to dangle awhile. Later,[37] he is pulled the rest of the distance, bound, and forced by Sylvia to promise her marriage. The resemblance, except in characters, hardly warrants Langbaine's assertion.[38]

His suggestion, however, brings better results when applied to a much earlier comedy. In Etherege's *Comical Revenge*, (1664) appear the characters of Sir Frederick, much the same mad-cap, harum-scarum wild gallant as Thomas, and the Widow Rich, parallel in character with Thomas' scornful mistress, Mary. Sir Frederick, like Thomas, is constantly refused by his mistress because of his waywardness; like Thomas he would enjoy the bodily delights of matrimony, without the chains; like Thomas he uses all sorts of devices to get access to his mistress. As Thomas serenades Mary, so Sir Frederick serenades the Widow, without effect.[39] At last he is brought in on a bier, as dead[40] and thus wins the widow from her domestic stronghold. But he is too precipitate and sure of his victory; consequently he loses his advantage.

This type of situation is very common in later Restoration comedy, and there is a strong probability that it owes its inception to the Beaumont and

[35] *Monsieur Thomas*, III, 3.
[36] *The Soldier's Fortune*, IV, 2.
[37] *The Soldier's Fortune*, V, 1.
[38] Op. cit., p. 399. "And that of Courtine at Sylvia's balcony like M. Thomas, his carriage to his mistress in that play of Fletcher's so-called."
[39] *The Comical Revenge*, III, 2 and 3.
[40] *Ibid*, IV, 7.

Fletcher play. As the later types of comedy drew farther away from the first decade of the Restoration, we find that the dramatists, building upon the foundation of their predecessors, developed the situation in a more intricate manner. In *The Comical Revenge,* however, one of the earliest of the new type, the resemblance to the Jacobean comedy is very strong.

4. Genest, speaking of Steele's *The Funeral,* (1702) asserts that "Lady Sharlots making of her escape in the coffin[41] is borrowed from *The Knight of the Burning Pestle.*[42]" It is true that this device is the same as that made use of by Luce and Jasper in the older play[43] but the parallelism of form and situation hardly warrants the classing of this as a borrowing. It is certainly probable, however, that Steele conceived the idea of using such a device from a reading or seeing of the old play.

5. There is a close similarity between a situation in Shadwell's *The Lancashire Witches* (1681) and one in Beaumont and Fletcher's *Wit at Several Weapons.* In the Jacobean play we have Sir Gregory Fop who has come to town to marry Oldcraft's niece, otherwise nameless. With Sir Gregory comes Cunningham, with whom the Niece falls in love. In Shadwell's comedy, Isabella, in love with Belfort, is required by her father to marry Sir Timothy Shacklehead, much the same sort of fool as Sir Gregory. The parallel now becomes more apparent. In the third act of *Wit at Several Weapons* the Niece, while her uncle is absent, flouts Sir Gregory, jeering at him in no ladylike terms. However, when the knight complains to Oldcraft, she puts on a complaisant air and denies everything, pretending to be quite willing to marry the fool. The same

---

[41] *The Funeral,* V, 1.
[42] Genest, p. 254, Vol. II.
[43] *Knight of the Burning Pestle,* IV, 4 and V, 3.

tactics are adopted by Isabella in Shadwell's play,[44] resulting in the same conclusion as that in the older comedy—i.e. both ladies escape their foolish lovers and marry the favored suitors. The chief difference between the two developments of the situation is that Shadwell, true to his methods, gives Isabella a command of billingsgate far surpassing that of the Niece.

Conclusion

These are only a few of the examples of imitation that might be cited. It would be possible, of course, to list a large number of situations and characters in Restoration comedy which "suggest" the Beaumont and Fletcher dramas,[45] and other borrowings and imitations have been suggested as appearing in certain plays.[46] But the few examples I have been able to discuss are important as proving that at least eleven (and probably many more) supposedly original Restoration plays are indebted to Beaumont and Fletcher for valuable situations, characters, or ideas. Nor is it true that these plays are by men who are hack writers only, and not true representatives of the Restoration spirit. Dryden,

[44] *The Lancashire Witches*, II, 1.

[45] For example a plusible case might be made out for relations between the underplot of Congreve's *The Old Bachelor* and Beaumont and Fletcher's *The Spanish Curate;* or between Edward Howard's *The Six Days' Adventure* and Beaumont and Fletcher's *The Sea Voyage.*

[46] Thus Genest states that Fletcher's *The Spanish Curate* was pillaged by Drake for his comedy, *The Sham Lawyer* (Genest, II, 113). Dyce adds (Works of B&F, VII, 4) ". . . that the second scene of the fourth act of Ravenscroft's *London Cuckolds* was suggested by the last scene of the second act of *Women Pleased.*" I have not seen a copy of Drake's comedy. Baker speaks of *The Triumphs of Virtue,* an anonymous tragi-comedy, the comic parts of which seem partly borrowed from Fletcher's *Wit Without Money.* (Biographia Dramatica.) Only by a long stretch of imagination is it possible to see any resemblance between *The London Cuckolds* and *Women Pleased.* There is a possible parallel between *Wit Without Money* and *The Triumphs of Virtue.* In the latter play, Antonio has wasted all his and his sister's wealth, much as Valentine, in *Wit Without Money* dissipated his own and his brother's inheritance. Antonio's lands are kept by his friend, Montano, cognate with the Uncle, in W. W. M. Both Antonio and Valentine, in their respective plays, are reformed, given money and clothes, and restored to their possessions.

Congreve, Etherege, Shadwell, Otway and D'Urfey are among the most important dramatists of the period.

To conclude: Our examination of alterations, borrowings and imitations has shown the following to be true:

1. That the Beaumont and Fletcher comedies were acceptable to the Restoration, unaltered or altered.

2. That the alterations of Beaumont and Fletcher comedies represent, not an attempt to render usable that which is no longer in agreement with contemporary tastes, but rather a deliberate theft of good material, sufficiently and capriciously disguised to prevent recognition by forgetful audiences.

3. That examples of deliberate borrowings by the younger dramatists from the older are sufficiently numerous to warrant the assumption that the Restoration followed Beaumont and Fletcher in several type situations.

4. That parallelisms of situation and characters support the last general conclusion and give rise to the warrantable generalization that the later dramatists regarded the comedies of Beaumont and Fletcher as excellent models. This, of course, is supported by the statistics which show how popular the works of the old dramatists were in the later period, and by the critical eulogies of Beaumont and Fletcher for wit and ingenuity, those characteristics which were so highly prized by the Restoration.

Then we should be able to find, in the two groups of comedies, still more parallelisms or likenesses in spirit, plot and characters. This is the task for our next chapter.

CHAPTER IV

BEAUMONT AND FLETCHER AND THE RESTORATION

THE PLAYS OF Beaumont and Fletcher may be grouped under three main headings as comedies, tragicomedies and tragedies. It is with the first two that we are concerned. Tragi-comedies must be admitted into our lists when they are of the type which contains two plots, one comic and one serious, or when they make use of comic devices in a serious setting. Reference, then, to a tragi-comedy will always be to the comic part of the play. It is often difficult with such a play, for example, as *The Humorous Lieutenant*, to determine whether it should be called comedy or tragi-comedy. Therefore we shall deal with comic elements, wherever found.

The pure comedies are the following: *The Captain, The Chances, The Custom of the Country, The Elder Brother, The Knight of the Burning Pestle, The Little French Lawyer, Love's Cure, The Maid in the Mill, The Noble Gentleman, Rule a Wife and Have a Wife, The Scornful Lady, The Sea Voyage, The Wild Goose Chase, Wit at Several Weapons, Wit Without Money, The Woman Hater*, and *The Woman's Prize*. All, with the single exception of *Love's Cure* must have been seen by the Restoration, and *The Chances, The Maid in the Mill, Rule a Wife and Have a Wife, The Scornful Lady, the Wild Goose Chase*, and *Wit Without Money* were seen quite frequently. In addition we must consider several of the mixed plays which we call tragi-comedies: *The Coxcomb, The Humorous Lieutenant,*

*Monsieur Thomas, The Night Walker, The Spanish
Curate, and Women Pleased. The Humorous Lieuten-
ant* and *The Spanish Curate* were well known in the
Restoration.[1]

The chief characters and plots of Restoration
comedy have been examined briefly, with the analysis
of one typical play.[2] I propose here to analyse the plot
and characteristics of *The Scornful Lady,* that comedy
by Beaumont and Fletcher which was undoubtedly
most popular in the Restoration.

Two plots are loosely linked together. The main
plot deals with the efforts of the Elder Loveless to
reinstate himself in the favor of his mistress, the Lady,
after he has publicly boasted of her favors. Their
conversation is both sophisticated and witty. Baffled
in his attempts to convince with logic, Loveless disguises himself as a returned traveler, and brings the
lady news that her lover has been drowned at sea.
His younger brother, a gay young rake, rejoices and
proceeds to waste his estate. The Lady is heartbroken
at first, but eventually she recognizes Loveless, and to
punish him announces her intention of marrying Welford, another suitor. Later, however, she rejects
Welford, who then conspires with Loveless. With Welford dressed as his bride, Loveless taunts his mistress
for her hardness of heart. She offers to marry him
at once. He accepts, and Welford, still disguised, is
left to go to bed with Martha, the Lady's younger
sister, whom he seduces. The next day, after much
obscene wit at the expense of the couple who have
anticipated their vows, they are hurried off to church.
The sub-plot, meanwhile, has dwelt on the working

---

[1] That type of melodrama which is represented by such plays as *A King
and No King,* I am not considering here; they are closely related to the Restoration Heroic play.

[2] See ante, p. 33ff.

out of relations between the younger Loveless, a rich widow whom he finally marries, and Morecraft, a usurer, whom he dupes, and who finally reforms.

Of these characters, Welford and the Loveless brothers represent the wild gallant in different stages of his evolution. The Lady is a sophisticated, emancipated woman; her sister and the widow are merely figures. Abigail, the maid, is a lecherous old creature, much smitten with Sir Roger, the household priest, whose name became a by-word with the Restoration audiences. Minor figures, the poet, the captain, and so forth, are conceived in something akin to the "humors" manner.

Wit is all important. The dialogue is not that of Congreve, certainly; it is nearer that of Dryden, broader, less epigrammatic, less polished than that of the author of *The Way of the World*. Occasionally the dialogue becomes as obscene as that of Tom D'Urfey; usually, however, it is both witty and obscene, that is to say, cleverly suggestive. There is no seriousness in the play, no consideration of contemporary problems. There is some satire of manners mingled with much intrigue, disguise and the like. The characters are not individualized as Shakespeare's are; they are the same types we find cropping up in the Beaumont and Fletcher plays over and over again. Noticeable at once, if we compare this play with Otway's *Friendship in Fashion*, briefly summarized before, is the absence of Otway's hard cynicism, his utter moral depravity. The authors of *The Scornful Lady* were cynical for their generation, and other plays bearing their names contain grosser immoralities, but the complete amorality of Otway is far beyond them.

But Otway's comedy represents the Restoration

drama at its height, in 1678.   Analysis of Dryden's
The Wild Gallant, produced in 1664, shows an entirely
different type of play representative of that time.
Briefly this is the plot:

Loveall, dunned for his lodging money, finds in his
pocket gold which has been placed there through the
efforts of his mistress, Lady Constance.³   Lady Constance has been commanded by her father to marry
Sir Timorous, but her impecunious cousin, Isabella,
wants the wealthy fop for herself.⁴   After a series of
disconnected and episodic adventures, trickeries, ar-
rests, suits and intrigues, Isabella succeeds in marrying Sir Timorous, and Lady Constance, in a setting
of mock spirits and devils, is married to Loveall.   The
plot is confused and chaotic; the characters are weakly
developed, but clearly in the later tradition; the wit is
coarse and broad, and the farce is of very low order.
The spirit of the play, while sophisticated, lacks the
coldness, the amoral tendency of later comedies; there
is about the play more of the Caroline roguery and
careless, fun-loving attitude toward life.

This play, which may be considered representative
of comedy at the beginning of the period, is as much
more naive than *The Scornful Lady,* as Otway's play
is more sophisticated.   In other ways, too, the earlier
plays of the Restoration are below the Beaumont and
Fletcher standard—not merely in excellence, but in
the working out of the intrigue manners tradition.   A
comparison of Etherege's play *The Comical Revenge*
with any of the Beaumont and Fletcher comedies, say
Monsieur Thomas, would show at once that Etherege
was experimenting with tools long used skillfully by
the older dramatists. And so with others of the first few

³ A situation paralleled in *Wit Without Money,* II, 2.
⁴ See a similar situation in *Wit at Several Weapons,* Acts IV and V.

years of the Restoration, always we find that the Beaumont and Fletcher comedies were more cynical, more
sophisticated, witty and obscene; their plots were better developed, their characters more fully defined;
their technique more effective. But in the middle and
late years of the Restoration, the opposite is true; the
later playwrights, having arrived at the stage of ad-
vancement represented by Beaumont and Fletcher,
proceeded to surpass those writers in nearly every
phase of their craft. I do not mean to imply, of course,
that a comedy by D'Urfey or Ravenscroft was neces-
sarily better than a comedy by Fletcher; rather that
even these two hack writers, working in a shop where
all the tools had been previously prepared, the materi-
als cut to pattern and the blue prints classified and
ordered, would have been poor workmen indeed if
their products had not been well done. And it must
be remembered, too, that most of the great names
of the Restoration belong to this later period. Wycherley's first play appeared in 1671, Congreve's in 1693,
Vanbrugh's in 1696 and Farquhar's in 1699. Etherege
and Dryden pioneered in the new comedy, but their
best work belongs to the later period.

The greatest influence of Beaumont and Fletcher
must have been exerted between the years 1660 and
1675, although it probably continued with diminishing
effect until the end of the century. I propose here to
point out the general resemblances between the comedies of Beaumont and Fletcher and those of their
successors.

Plots

Generally the comic plots of the two older dramatists consist of a series of adventures, farcial, romantic, or more frequently erotic. Such a play as *The*

Noble Gentleman is farce from beginning to end, farce, however, which is tinged with sensuality. *The Maid in the Mill* is in part a story of romantic love, partly farce and partly sex-intrigue (using the term in its lowest sense). The very popular *Rule a Wife and Have a Wife* has a double plot, one of the gulling farce type, so common with the early Jacobean dramatists in general, and one a rather luscious sex plot, dealing with intrigue, cuckolding and the like. The humorous part of the play, *Monsieur Thomas,* is the story of the escapades of a young rake, who leaps gaily from one erotic situation to another. Like the Restoration comedies, nearly all of Beaumont and Fletcher's comic dramas have as their foundation the combat between the sexes, which may result in marriage, fornication or adultery. It has already been pointed out that the comedies of the Restoration abound in stock plots and situations, and a few of the commonest of these have been cited. We shall see that many of the same situations are treated in similar ways by Beaumont and Fletcher.

1. The bringing of a woman hater to his knees is the main theme of Beaumont and Fletcher's *The Woman Hater* and *The Captain.* The characters in these two comedies are men who hate, not merely marriage, but women in general. If we seek for gentlemen who hate marriage but are nevertheless libertines, we have not far to search. Mirabel, in *The Wild Goose Chase,* Hylas and Thomas in *Monsieur Thomas,* Don John, in *The Chances,* Marc-Antonio, in *Love's Pilgrimage,* and a dozen others belong in this category. Such characters are not uncommon in the general run of pre-Restoration comedy, but the cynicism of the Beaumont and Fletcher heroes comes nearer to that of the Restoration fine gentlemen. Compare, for ex-

ample, the statement of Lovely, in Crowne's *The Married Beau*:

He that debauches a fine woman, conquers her; but if a beauty makes me marry her, 'egad, she conquers me.[5]

with the following passage from *The Wild Goose Chase*:

ORIANA. Do you not love me then?
MIRABEL. As I love others; heartily I love thee;
   When I am high and lusty, I love thee cruelly:
   After I have made a plenteous meal and satisfied
   My senses with all delicates, come to me,
   And thou shalt see how I love thee.
ORIANA. Will you not marry me?
MIRABEL. No, certain, no, for anything I know yet:
   I must not lose my liberty, dear lady,
   And like a wanton slave cry for more shackles.[6]

and, for neat cynicism, add this from *Monsieur Thomas*:

THOMAS. Thou never meanst then,
   To marry any that thou lov'st?
HYLAS. No, surely;
   Nor any wise man, I think. Marriage!
   Would you have me now begin to be 'prentice
   And learn to cobble other men's old boots?
THOMAS. Why, you may take a maid.
HYLAS. Where? Can you tell me?
   Or if it were possible I might get a maid,
   To what use should I put her? look upon her?
   Dandle her upon my knee and give her sugar sops?[7]

2. Lovers counterfeiting some physical ailment to get the sympathy of mistress or servant are not so common. Monsieur Thomas, in the play by that name, pretends to have broken his leg.[8]; Loveless, in *The Scornful Lady*, feigns death;[9] and Oriana, in *The Wild*

---

[5] *The Married Beau*, II, 1,.
[6] *The Wild Goose Chase*, II, 1.
[7] *Monsieur Thomas*, II, 3.
[8] *Ibid*, III, 3.
[9] *The Scornful Lady*, III, 1.

Goose Chase, pretends madness, with little effect upon her lover, Mirabel.[10]   These are, however, merely specific examples of that type of situation common to both groups of comedies, that in which the lover attempts to gain the sympathy and love of a hard-hearted mistress, or to get access to a mistress who is carefully guarded.   Thus, just as Leandro, in *The Spanish Curate,* feigns a desire to be a lawyer, in order to seduce Bartolus' wife,[11] so Bellamy, in Dryden's *An Evening's Love,* pretends to be an astrologer in order to gain the favor of Don Alonzo, an amateur, and so be admitted to Don Alonzo's daughter.[12]   Or again, Monsieur Thomas disguises himself as a woman in order to lie with his mistress, Mary,[13] and, to carry out the parallel, Townly, in D'Urfey's *Sir Barnaby Whigg,* disguises as a woman in order to visit his mistress, Livia.[14]   More such parallels might be cited, but these are sufficient to show that the two groups of comedies deal in similar ways with common intrigue situations.   The only way in which the Restoration differed from Beaumont and Fletcher was in a tendency to treat these situations in a more farcical manner.

3.   The device of disguise, that is, the dressing of women in men's clothing, is very popular in Restoration comedy.   This, of course, was very popular before the Restoration; the disguised damsels appeared in all sorts of comedies and tragi-comedies.   Shakespeare's famous heroines are good examples.   But the comic heroines of Beaumont and Fletcher differ greatly from the romantic ladies of Shakespeare and others; they are nearer the Restoration type in their matter-of-fact unconventionality, their gay spirit of intrigue, and

[10] *The Wild Goose Chase,* IV, 3.
[11] *The Spanish Curate,* II, 2.
[12] *An Evening's Love,* II, 3.
[13] *Monsieur Thomas,* IV, 3.
[14] *Sir Barnaby Whigg,* IV, 2.

their complete lack of morality. To come to concrete examples, we have, in *Love's Cure,* a heroine who is more gifted at fighting than at love making, and who wins her lover from the blandishments of a prostitute by the strength of her good right arm. Shadwell's heroine in *The Woman Captain* and D'Urfey's in *Madam Fickle* are of the same type. In Beaumont and Fletcher's *The Night Walker,* we have Alathe, who puts on boys' clothes to raise mischief generally; Alinda, in *The Pilgrim* wears breeches to escape from her father; Lady Ruinous, in *Wit at Several Weapons,* disguises as a man to commit robbery. These are examples from comedy only; we are not dealing here with the romantic heroines, who are far more numerous.

In the Restoration the disguising of women as boys or men for the purposes of comic intrigue is too common to require elaboration. They become rakes and make love to their own sex;[15] they further love plots of their own;[16] they pursue their lovers, or perhaps, serve them as pages.[17] In fact, it is difficult to find comedies which do not contain some variant of this device. This comic heroine is a very wild and wanton lady usually; rarely, in comedy, does she belong to the group of self-sacrificing, sincere, love-sick girls of extreme morality, best represented by Beaumont and Fletcher's Ballario in *Philaster.* Yet there is certainly the possibility that much of the impetus toward the Restoration use of the disguised girl in comedy may have come as well from the serious plays of the two Jacobeans as from their comedies. They made use of so many variations upon the conventional device that

---

[15] Southerne, *Sir Anthony Love.*

[16] Crowne, *The Athiest.*

[17] Wycherley *The Plain Dealer,* Farquhar *The Inconstant, Love and a Bottle.* Shadwell, *Bury Fair.*

it seems almost impossible for the Restoration to have gone beyond them.[18]

4. Rarely does a Restoration comedy end without a marriage, and often the intrigue is so confused that it results in strange matches, to the confusion of the unhappy participants. This situation, too, was made use of by Beaumont and Fletcher. In *Wit at Several Weapons* Sir Gregory marries Mirabel, under the impression that she is his true mistress.[19] In *The Captain*, Lelia, a reformed courtezan, is married to Piso by trickery.[20] In *The Maid in the Mill*, Martine, endeavoring to marry Ismenia, is deceived by Aminta, who thinks she is marrying Antonio, and the two deceivers find themselves united to each other.[21] In *The Noble Gentleman* Maria tricks Beaufort into marrying her.[22] Such situations, often still more complicated, are common in Restoration comedy. Perhaps the most famous is that in Congreve's *Love for Love*,[23] in which Mrs. Frail and Tattle are married to each other in disguise, each thinking the other to be some one else. This is parallel to the example cited from *The Maid in the Mill*.

There are many other episodic situations in Restoration comedy for which parallels may be found in the work of Beaumont and Fletcher. The situation in which a lover makes his mistress jealous by pretending marriage with or love for another woman,[24] that in which a country gentleman comes to town to

---

[18] For example, in *The Double Marriage* a page is so drawn as to deceive the audience into the belief that he is a disguised girl. When he appears in women's clothing, the belief becomes certainty. But he is stripped and found to be a boy in fact.

[19] *Wit at Several Weapons*, V. 1.

[20] *The Captain*, V. 5.

[21] *The Maid in the Mill,*, IV, 3.

[22] *The Noble Gentleman*, IV, 5.

[23] *Love for Love*, V, 1.

[24] See *The Scornful Lady* and Durfey's *The Modern Prophets*.

marry a lady and finds her disdainful of him,[25] marriage for money followed by the discovery that neither
party to the contract is wealthy,[26] the many variants
upon the cuckolding situation,[27]—all these are common
in the Restoration and can be paralleled in at least one,
if not more of Beaumont and Fletcher's comedies. The
fact remains, of course, that they may be found in
other Jacobean dramas also; yet the Restoration knew
best the work of the two collaborators, and little of
the dramas of their contemporaries.

Enough examples have been cited to show that in
subject matter the Restoration agreed with Beaumont
and Fletcher in finding certain types of situations interesting. We must remember that, after all, Restoration comedy in the hands of any dramatist, was merely
a variation of one of two plots: that dealing with the
pursuit of a man by a woman, or that dealing with the
pursuit of a woman by a man, for holy or unholy purposes. Even the farce-gulling comedies must have
such a plot as a ground work. The Beaumont and
Fletcher comedies are based upon the same plots, and
the variants used by them and by the Restoration
writers are so often parallel as to suggest that the
later writers were led to follow the older dramatists,
as a result of seeing those variant situations successful upon the stage. This conclusion, of course, is
supported by our previous analysis of important borrowings and imitations.

Characteristic Tone

In spirit, also, the Restoration comedy shows many
likenesses to that of Beaumont and Fletcher. Cynical
gaiety is certainly a distinguishing mark of the late
seventeenth century comedy, and, while Beaumont and

[25] See *Rule a Wife and Have a Wife* and D'Urfey's *The Boarding School.*
[26] See *Wit at Several Weapons* and Farquhar's *Love and a Bottle.*
[27] See almost any comedy, old or new.

Fletcher's comedies are often romantic in tone, certain of them—notably *The Scornful Lady, The Chances, Rule a Wife and Have a Wife, The Wild Goose Chase, The Spanish Curate* and *Wit Without Money*—express in the gayest terms the dramatists' disregard for morality, their disbelief in the virtue of women and the honesty of men, their extreme sophistication. And these were the plays most popular on the later stage. It is difficult to cite specific examples of that which is spread out over entire plays; the consideration of attitudes common to the two groups of plays offers more opportunity for citation.

1. The Restoration attitude toward marriage as the last resort of the worn out or impoverished rake, as a prison for gentlemen and an opportunity for women to be promiscuous is too well known to require examples. It has already been shown that Beaumont and Fletcher shared this attitude, or rather, were among the first to express an idea which became conventionalized. It is an attitude common enough with Jacobean and Caroline dramatists, not unknown even to the writers of the late sixteenth century, but the expression given to it by Beaumont and Fletcher is peculiarly cynical. With them the masculine attitude toward marriage is no longer the off-hand pronouncement found, say, in Middleton's comedies; it has become a subject for infinite jest, for elaborate and drawn out conceits. And the complementary attitude, that of women toward marriage and sex, we find nowhere so clearly expressed as in their comedies.[28]

[28] We have, it is true, such plays as Marston's *The Insatiate Countess,* but this, be it noted, is a tragic treatment of the subject. In general, in the predecessors of Fletcher and Beaumont, sex irregularity is treated either as a subject for tragedy, or farcical device in low comedy. See, for example, Middleton's *A Chaste Maid in Cheapside,* Dekker's *The Honest Whore,* or Heywood's *A Woman Killed with Kindness.* In the same way incest, tragically treated by Ford in *'Tis Pity She's a Whore,* becomes a subject for romantic comedy in Beaumont and Fletcher's *A King and No King.*

Here, for example, is a passage from *Rule a Wife and Have a Wife,* which expresses the attitude of the women in Restoration comedy as surely as that of Beaumont and Fletcher's heroine. Margarita has been asking advice of two old ladies. She wishes to marry, partly that her husband may take care of her estate, and partly that she may be left to follow her amorous desires:

FIRST LADY. Do you find your body so malicious that way?
MARGARITA. I find it as all bodies are that are young and lusty,
　　　　　　Lazy and high-fed; I desire my pleasure,
　　　　　　And pleasure I must have.
SECOND LADY. 'Tis fit you should have;
　　　　　　Your years require it and 'tis necessary,
　　　　　　As necessary as meat to a young lady;
　　　　　　Sleep cannot nourish more.
FIRST LADY. But might not all this be had and keep you single?
　　　　　　You take away variety in marriage,
　　　　　　The abundance of the pleasure you are barred then:
　　　　　　Is't not abundance that you aim at?
MARGARITA. Yes;
　　　　　　Why was I made a woman?
SECOND LADY. And every day a new?
MARGARITA. Why fair and young but to use it?
SECOND LADY. You are still i' the right; why would you marry
　　　　　　then?
ALTHEA (the maid) Because a husband stops all doubts in this
　　　　　　point
　　　　　　And clears all passages.[29]

Here is, indeed, a neat summary of the ladies' philosophy. It is a clear declaration, from the brutal first speech to the double meaning of the last. The Restoration could hardly improve upon it.

2. Cynical frankness on matters of sex, apart from marriage, was as common in both groups of comedies with women as with men. It is hardly necessary to cite examples of masculine openness, from either group, and, unfortunately, feminine discussions of sex

---

[29] *Rule a Wife and Have a Wife,* II, 1.

are often unquotable. But the common attitude of the
ladies toward discussions of the forbidden may be
shown by one or two quotations. From Beaumont and
Fletcher's *The Wild Goose Chase,* we select this as an
example:

LILLIA BIANCA. Pinac, methinks, is reasonable;
    A little modesty he has brought home with him,
    And might be taught in time some handsome duty.
ROSALURA. They say he is a wencher, too.
LILLIA BIANCA. I like him better;
    A free light touch or two becomes a gentleman,
    And sets him seemly off: so he exceed not,
    But keep his compass clear, he may be looked at.
    I would not marry a man that must be taught,
    And conjured up with kisses; the best game
    Is played still by the best gamesters.
ROSULURA. Fie upon thee!
    What talk hast thou!
LILLIA BIANCA. Are not we alone, and merry?
    Why should we be ashamed to speak what we think? [30]

And in Etherege's *She Would if She Could,* when Gatty
has finished singing a loose song, her sister chides her:

ARIANA. Fie, sister! thou art so wanton.
GATTY. I hate to dissemble when I need not; 'twould look as
    affected in us to be reserved now we're alone, as for a
    player to maintain the character she acts in the tiring
    room. [31]

Or add this, from Duffett's *The Spanish Rogue:*

LEONELLA. This idle peevish thing called modesty,
    Is woman's most invet'rate enemy:
    Lay it aside, none but ourselves are here,
    Blushes are vain when none but women hear. [32]

---

[30] *The Wild Goose Chase,* III, 1. Compare with this passage from Mount-
fort's *Greenwich Park,* Act II, i.
VIOLANTE. Fie, how you talk!
FLORELLA. Fie, how I talk! Why you think the same, and so does the whole
    sex.
VIOLANTE. Have you no regard to virtue?
FLORELLA. Yes, as long as Virtue has any regard to me. Prithee let us not
    affect that nicety when we're alone which we assume in Publick.
[31] *She Would If She Could,* V, 1.
[32] *The Spanish Rogue,* II, 2.

3. These two attitudes, toward marriage and sex, are the most important to be found in either group of comedies, which, we must bear constantly in mind, dealt chiefly, if not exclusively, with the battle between the sexes. That they are cynical attitudes is sufficiently obvious. Clear also is that subtle obscenity of phrase and situation that caused Lovelace to say of Beaumont and Fletcher's plays:

> View here a loose thought said with such a grace
> Minerva might have spoke in Venus' face.[33]

The Restoration critic and dramatist, Flecknoe, in 1664, expressed it more baldly:

> Beaumont and Fletcher were excellent in their kind, but they often erred against decorum, seldom representing a man without something of the braggadocio, nor an honorable woman without something of the Doll Common about her; besides, Fletcher was the first who introduced that witty obscenity in his plays which like poison infused in pleasant liquor is always the more dangerous, the more delightful.[34]

Perhaps this emphasis on "witty obscenity" explains in large measure the popularity of the Beaumont and Fletcher comedies in the Restoration.[35] Unquestionably this is the sort of thing the Restoration loved. Although other pre-Restoration dramatists dealt in obscenity it was of a different type, frank vulgarity with the majority of the Elizabethans, and very mild wickedness with the minor Caroline and Jacobean playwrights. It is the obscene repartee which the Restoration prized in the Beaumont and Fletcher comedies.[36] However, this in itself is not enough to prove an

---

[33] Commendatory poems prefixed to the 1647 Folio.

[34] Quoted by Spingarn, *Critical Essays of the Seventeenth Century*, II, 93.

[35] Cf. Davies, Dramatic Miscellanies, 1783, II, 392: "To this freedom of style they in some measure owed the success of their dramas in the reign of Charles the Second. They approached nearer in dialogue and character to the color of the times, than the plays of any other author."

[36] Cf. Baker, D. E., *Biographia Dramatica* (1782) I, p. 18.

influence. But what are we to say when we find Dryden, smarting under Collier's attack, declaring that "there is more bawdry in one play of Fletcher's called *The Custom of the Country*, than in all ours together."[37] And Mrs. Behn, defending herself against the charge of obscenity, maintains that she is following good examples:

> So in that lucky play of *The London Cuckolds* not to recite particulars. And in that good comedy of *Sir Courtly Nice* [39] the tailor to the young lady—in the famed Sir Fopling,[40] Doriman and Belinda, see the very words—in *Valentian*,[41] see the scene between the court bawds. And Valentinian all loose and ruffled a moment after the rape, and all this you see without scandal, and a thousand others; the *Moor of Venice*,[42] in many places. *The Maid's Tragedy*,[43] see the scene of undressing the bride, and between the king and Amintor, and after, between the king and Evadne, all these I name as some of the best plays I know.[44]

Dryden exaggerated very little. Certainly *The Custom of the Country* contains several scenes which are decidedly strong,[45] the most pornographic of which, however, was that taken over and amplified upon by Cibber in his alteration of the play. But this latter must not be taken as an indication that the Restoration preferred disguised obscenity and objected to frank exposition of sex relations. It liked, no doubt, such things as the famous China Scene in Wycherley's *The Country Wife*, but it liked also bawdy houses, bedroom scenes, and all that belongs thereto. Beaumont and Fletcher furnished both types, and Mrs. Behn

[37] Prefare to *The Fables.*
[38] Ravenscroft, 1681.
[39] Crowne, 1685.
[40] *The Man of Mode*, Etherege, 1676.
[41] Beaumont and Fletcher.
[42] *Othello.*
[43] Beaumont and Fletcher.
[44] Preface to *The Lucky Chance*, 1686.
[45] Particularly Act I, 2; II, 2; and IV, 4.

might have cited many more examples as authority for her own practise. Certainly it is true that the comedies of the two collaborators were very close to those of the Restoration in open obscenity and clever suggestiveness—a doubtful honor. But it is far from my purpose to prove that the Restoration was led into the pathways of vice by the wicked Jacobeans; the court of Charles II needed no tempters. I wish to show, rather, that the method used by Beaumont and Fletcher is that adopted by their successors. What that method is will become clearer in the sequel.

4. The Restoration prided itself upon its wit, without being careful to define what it meant by that quality, often, indeed, confusing it with invention. To judge by the plays themselves, there were really two types of wit: that brilliant, scintillating, epigrammatic "coterie talk" for which Etherege and Congreve are justly famous, and the much commoner sort which appeared in dialogue as a series of broad or subtle jests, thinly disguised sarcasms, fantastic nonsense and clever bawdry. All this was included under the general title of repartee—that for which Beaumont and Fletcher were praised by the Restoration. Thus we find Dryden saying:

And as for comedy, repartee is one of its chiefest graces, the greatest pleasure of an audience is the chase of wit, kept up on both sides and swiftly managed. And this our forefathers, if not we, have had in Fletcher's plays to a much higher degree of perfection than the French poets can reasonably hope to reach . . . . they understood and imitated the conversation of gentlemen much better, whose wild debaucheries and quickness of wit in repartee, no poet before them could paint as they have done.

The clue to an understanding of Restoration wit is in the last two statements: "wild debaucheries" and "quickness of wit in repartee." This is not the pol-

[46] *Essay of Dramatic Poesy* (ed. Mitford), p. 238.

ished play upon universals that we find in the work of
Congreve. It is personal, pointed, debauched.

Examples of such wit in Beaumont and Fletcher are
not hard to find, but are usually too long to quote. We
find the badinage of witty lovers, surely one of the
distinguishing marks of Restoration comedy, ably represented in *The Scornful Lady*,[47] or in *Wit Without
Money*,[48] to name two plays well known after the
period of the commonwealth. Or, for a short quotation, this, from *The Wild Goose Chase*:

Enter Mirabel, to Lillia Bianca and Rosalura.

MIRABEL. Bless ye, sweet beauties, sweet incomparable ladies,
        Sweet wits, sweet humors, bless you learned lady!
        And you, most holy nun, bless your devotions!
LILLIA. And bless your brains, sir, your most pregnant brains,
                                                        sir!
        They are in travel; may they be delivered
        Of a most hopeful wild goose!
ROSALURA. Bless your manhood!
        They say you are a gentleman of action,
        A fair accomplished man, and a rare engineer;
        You have a rare trick to blow up maidenheads,
        A subtle trick, they say abroad.
MIRABEL. I have, lady.
ROSALURA. And often glory in their ruins.
MIRABEL. Yes, forsooth;
        I have a speedy trick, please you to try it;
        My engine will despatch you instantly.[49]

It would be redundant here to point out at length the
personal applications of wit, the free, wild frankness,
and even the tone of unreality, that tone which caused
Charles Lamb to plead, in his defense of Restoration
comedy, that it lived in a world of its own. To this
quotation we may add another which illustrates a
definite quality of wit; its double meaning, which may

[47] *The Scornful Lady*, I, 1.
[48] *Wit Without Money*, II, 1.
[49] *The Wild Goose Chase*, III, 1.

be merely smutty, or may be the clever fencing with words between two antagonists who mean more than they say and are quite aware of each other's real desires. In a scene from *Wit Without Money* we have the meeting of two lovers, Isabella and Francisco; the latter pleads his love with passionate eagerness:

ISABELLA. This is a pretty riot!
          It may grow to a rape.
FRANCISCO. Do you like that better?
          I can ravish you a hundred times and never hurt you.
ISABELLA. Are you in earnest, sir? Do you long to be hanged?
FRANCISCO. Yes, by my troth, lady, in these fair tresses.
ISABELLA. Shall I call out for help?
FRANCISCO. No, by no means; that were a weak trick, lady; I'll
          kiss and stop your mouth. (Kisses her)
ISABELLA. You'll answer all these?
FRANCISCO. A thousand kisses more.[50]

This is double meaning gallantry verging on rape, if the term may be used with such ladies as Isabella. In a later comedy, Vanbrugh's *The Relapse*, the situation is worked out in much the same manner to a conclusion more shameless. The two situations are not identical in matter, but the same method is used in each. To quote from the Restoration comedy:

(*Loveless has come to Berinthia's chamber with proposals*)
BERINTHIA. Why, do you intend to make me blush?
LOVELESS. Faith, I can't tell that, but if I do, it shall be in the
          dark. (Pulling her)
BERINTHIA. O heavens! I would not be in the dark with you
          for all the world.
LOVELESS. I'll try that. (Puts out the candles)
BERINTHIA. Oh Lord! are you mad; what shall I do for light?
LOVELESS. You'll do well without it.
BERINTHIA. Why, one can't find a chair to sit down?
LOVELESS. Come into the closet, madam, there's moonshine upon
          the couch.
BERINTHIA. Nay, never pull, for I will not go.

[50] *Wit Without Money*, V, 3.

LOVELESS. Then you must be carried. (Carrying her)
BERINTHIA. Help, help, I'm ravished, ruin'd, undone. O Lord,
    I shall never be able to bear it. (Very softly) [51]

Certainly Vanbrugh went to extents that Beaumont
and Fletcher attempted only occasionally; yet his method, that of the "witty obscenity" is the same as theirs.
And it is this method that must have been of great
influence upon the comic writers of the Restoration.

Characters

The most characteristic figures of Restoration comedy are undoubtedly the witty lovers, gentlemen and
ladies. There may be one, two or even more such
couples. In addition we have the stock figures of the
lascivious maid servant, the eager old lady, the doting
or jealous guardian or father, the jealous or cuckolded
husband, and, trailing on down to minor farce figures,
the fop, the gull, the guller, the bully and the fool. Of
these, unquestionably, the lovers are most important.
From their actions the plot of the play develops; from
their characters the play takes its tone. The whole
period of the Restoration might well be symbolized by
these two figures, stock types in comedy.

1. Although it is certainly true that these characters
were occasionally caricatures of actual personages, and
that there is a strong resemblance between them and
their prototypes in the court of Charles II—the
Rochesters, Buckinghams, Sedleys, Stuarts, Castle-
maines and others—yet they are so artificialized and
standardized in the whole period of this drama as to
preclude the possibility of their being actual portraits.
Always they are stock figures; their names, even, are
used over and over again with so little variation in
character that one is constantly amazed at the lack of
change.

[51] *The Relapse*, IV, 3.

The history of this amorous pair on the Restoration stage has been variously claimed as beginning with Etherege's Sir Frederick and the Widow Rich in *The Comical Revenge,* (1664) and with Dryden's Loveall and Lady Constance, in *The Wild Gallant* (1663). But an earlier example of the type in embryo may be noted in Sir Robert Howard's *The Committee* (1662). Colonels Careless and Blunt conform to the tenets of the wild gallant, and their respective mistresses, Arbella and Ruth, are equally wild young ladies. Of the two men, Careless, especially, is as impudent, wild, lascivious and witty as womanly heart could wish.

A claim might also be made for Killigrew's Careless and Wild in *The Parson's Wedding* (circa 1660), as typical gallants, but these young gentlemen are too much in the tradition of Chapman. They are wild, they are somewhat witty, but they are gullers, sharpers, and not polished, cynical gentlemen in the Restoration sense. Like Brome's or Shirley's gallants, they are not sufficiently sophisticated; there is about them the touch of the prodigal son, whose reformation is only a matter of time.

With whatever comedy the wild couple may have first appeared, it is certainly true that their development was rapid, from the crude, weakly drawn figures of Careless, Loveall, and Sir Frederick, Arbella, Constance and the Widow Rich, to the full vigor of Etherege's Courtall and Freeman, Gatty and Ariana, in *She Would if She Could* (1668). By the end of the first decade of the Restoration, the type was well established, and it continued with little change until the eighteenth century wave of reform dulled its colors and inhibited its freedom. After all, Charles Surface is only a faded echo of the Restoration gallant, and Lady Teazle is the Restoration lady grown stout.

But this early period of development for the characters with which we are dealing was also the period of greatest popularity for the Beaumont and Fletcher dramas. Is it logical to reason that in characters, as in wit and cynicism, the Restoration first modeled on Beaumont and Fletcher, at last surpassing those dramatists? But let us see how nearly akin the wild couple of the Restoration is to the Beaumont and Fletcher hero and heroine.

The character of the Restoration gallant runs the gamut from what is almost morality on the one end to what is decided wickedness at the other. Valentine, the hero of Congreve's *Love for Love*, is a polished, witty gentleman, who has sown his wild oats and practically reformed. Mellefont, of the same writer's *The Double Dealer*, has scruples of honor which cause him much trouble. He is chiefly interested in getting safely married. Sir Harry Wildair, of Farquhar's *The Constant Couple*, is a dissolute ruffian of elegant deportment, who prefers illicit love, but has no objection to marriage if there is a good sized fortune to boot. Willmore, of Mrs. Behn's *The Rover*, is a thoroughly unprincipled rake who enters matrimony in such a casual way that we are sure he does not intend to remain long in the married state—nor does he. Horner, of Wycherley's *The Country Wife*, is a high priest of Venus and a scorner of Hymen. As his name indicates, matrimony is for him only a game preserve. Among these types can be placed all the witty gallants of Restoration comedy. Often two or more gallants, appearing in the same comedy, will differ in character; that is, one rake will be honestly bent on marriage, perhaps, while another will be occupied with illicit love only. A broad survey of the comedy of the period shows that these two types predominate.

The ladies who flirt, intrigue and perhaps lie with these gallants, vary also in the degree of their morality. Angelica, Valentine's beloved, is emancipated but physically innocent. Cynthia, whom Mellefont is so eager to marry, persists in maintaining her virginity intact, but is decidedly unshockable. Two ladies are concerned with Sir Harry Wildair: Angelica, a pure and innocent child, who, however, is willing to marry Sir Harry in spite of his past and her failure to love him, and Lady Lurewell, who is a prostitute in all but deed. Willmore's beloved, Hellena, would willingly have become his mistress, had he refused to marry her, and Horner's seraglio, Mrs. Pinchwife, Lady Fidget and the rest, are merely whores of high degree.

At worst, however, there is always one decent woman in every comedy and sometimes two. Usually, also, there is at least one man who is not a confirmed wencher. In that most obscene play, Vanbrugh's *The Relapse*, the great moral strength of Amanda is heightened by, and in turn sets off the depravity of her cousin, Berinthia; and in the same way Loveless' character is placed in opposition to that of Worthy, who, although for long in pursuit of Amanda, is finally reformed by her and becomes most impertinently moral. This method of heightening by contrast, as we shall see, was used very effectively by Beaumont and Fletcher.

It is important to dwell at some length upon the characteristics of the Restoration wild couple, for they form the chief link in the chain of our connections between the old drama and the new.

The best brief characterization of the wild gallant is, perhaps, that delivered by Mrs. Sullen, in Farquhar's *The Beaux Stratagem*. Speaking of her new lover, Archer, she says:

The devil's in this fellow! He fights, loves and banters, all
in a breath! [52]

Sir Harry Wildair, hero of *The Constant Couple* sum-
marizes his philosophy thus:

> I make the most of life, no hour miss-spend,
> Pleasure's the means, and pleasure is my end.
> No spleen, no trouble shall my time destroy;
> Life's but a span, I'll every inch enjoy.[53]

And like a gay ephemera the gallant dances through
life, leaving behind him a trail of duels and broken
hearts, until he is caught finally in the toils of marriage. Love is his whole business in life, the sort of
love described by Modely, in Johnson's *The Country
Lasses*:

> I love the whole sex, sir; the beautiful I adore as angels, the
> ugly as Indians do the devil, for fear; the witty persuade me, the
> proud raise my ambition, and the humble my charity; the coquet
> shows me a pretty chase, the false virtue of the prude gives
> oil to my flame, and the good-natured girl quenches it—there's
> a pleasure in pursuing those that fly, and 'tis cowardly not to
> meet the fair one that advances: say what you will, I am in love,
> in love, old boy, from head to foot. I am Cupid's butt and
> stand ready to receive his whole quiver.[54]

Raines, a character in Shadwell's *Epsom Wells*, expresses the matter more cynically when his friend
Woodly suggests that he visit the latter's cousin:

> Prithee, Woodly, what shall I do with her? I love thee and
> thy family too well to lie with her; and I think a man has no ex-
> cuse for himself that visits a woman without a design of lying
> with her one way or another.[55]

Raines is assuredly a gentleman, if we are to follow
the definition of that creature given by Sir Signal
Buffoon in Mrs. Behn's *The Feign'd Curtezans*:

[52] *The Beaux' Stratagem*, V, 4.
[53] *The Constant Couple*, II, 5.
[54] *The Country Lasses*, II, 2.
[55] *Epsom Wells*, I, 1.

Madam! A gentleman! Why, madam, they're the very monsters of the nation, they devour every day a virgin.[56]

The wild gallant has little respect for law and decorum, for marriage or virgin chastity. Drinking and venery contend for first place in his affections. Will Rant, chief of the scowrers in Shadwell's *The Scowrers*, makes a fine art of drinking and roistering, bullying and window breaking. His follower, Tope, is moved to enthusiasm:

My dear knight. My dear Will Rant, thou art the prince of drunkards and of scowrers; thou art a noble scavenger, and every night thou clearest the streets of scoundrel bullies and of idle rascals, and of all ale toasts and sops in brandy.[57]

But Will Rant is also a good deal of a wencher, and a rather unrefined wooer of his mistress.

Although it was the tradition that the wild gallant and his lady should marry at last, no reformation was demanded of either party, although certain stipulations might be laid down by each for the other to observe. In the newer drama of sentimentalism, which overlapped Restoration comedy toward the close of the century, reforms took place. Cibber, prophet of the new era, felt obliged to apologize in the epilogue to *Love's Last Shift* for such a reformation:

> Now, Sirs, to you, whose sole religion's drinking,
> Whoring, roaring, without the pain of thinking,
> I fear he's made a fault you'll ne'er forgive,
> A crime beyond the hopes of a reprieve;
> An honest rake forego the joys of life,
> His whores and wine, to embrace a dull chaste wife!
> Such out of fashion stuff! But then, again,
> He's lewd for above four acts, gentlemen.

How the fashion has shifted since Dryden, bringing out in 1667 his revised version of *The Wild Gallant*,

[56] *The Feign'd Curtezans,* IV, 1.
[57] *The Scrowrers,* I, 1.

apologized for not having made his hero wicked enough at first! But Cibber was a bit too early. Vanbrugh's famous play, *The Relapse*, represents Cibber's hero turning again to the traditional wickedness of his class.

The wild gallant is always a gentleman by birth, frequently wealthy, often poverty stricken. In the latter case he marries for money, or, like Loveall in Dryden's *The Wild Gallant*, or Freeman in Mrs. Behn's *The Roundheads*, has no compunction about accepting money from his mistress. He is witty always, sometimes with that type of wit which we should call low cunning, that which in Elizabethan comedy is the peculiar property of the gulling servant. Thus he often lives by his wits. " 'Sheart," says Sir Sampson to his son, Valentine, in Congreve's *Love for Love*, "Live by your wits—you were always fond of the wits:—now let's see if you have wit enough to keep yourself." [58] And Valentine shortly persuades his father that he has, even if his living must be made at the expense of his father's pocketbook.

The wild gallant has no religion. He pays his debts when he has the money and feels like it. He pursues women with perfunctory pleasure, breaks windows and receives memorials from grateful glaziers, beats the watch, and, almost as a matter of duty, makes extravagant love to the "impudent, ill-bred tom-rig" who is his mistress. He often has a friend or confident, a slightly lesser rascal than himself, who assists him in

---

[58] *Love for Love*, II, 1. And see Sir Perfidious Old-Craft to his son, Wittypate, in Beaumont and Fletcher's *Wit at Several Weapons* (I, 1)
    "If I can see thee thrive by
    Thy wits while I live, I shall have the more courage
    To trust thee with my lands when I die."
Wittypate is turned out to shift for himself, but he gulls his father and is given an allowance.

his intrigues and is usually rewarded with the hand of a lesser female character.

Just as there are two main types of wild gallants, so there are two of the emancipated ladies. The "ill-bred tom-rig" may be and frequently is just what her name implies, a romping hoyden with no regard for virtue or convention. She may pursue a man with insatiable eagerness, willing, like Belinda in Etherege's *The Man of Mode,* to be his mistress if she cannot marry him. Her frankness is often startling. Harriet, in the play just mentioned, who has succeeded in winning Dorimant from his old flame, Loveit, assures the latter that: "Mr. Dorimant has been your God Almighty long enough; 'tis time to think of another." [59] Yet Harriet is supposedly a lady, and she plans to marry Dorimant. While she is frank, however, another of these wild ladies may be coy and hypocritical, burning with eagerness for the joys of love, yet discussing her desires only with her feminine confidant. She may be, like Olivia in Wycherley's *The Plain Dealer,* a promiscuous hypocrite, or like Lady Fancy in Mrs. Behn's *Sir Patient Fancy,* many times an adulteress, but always she is a fine lady, well-mannered and witty.

On the other hand the wild lady may be merely an "emancipated" woman, whose virginity is preserved, whose chief concern in life is to get a husband, and who therefore fishes in the dangerous river of immorality in hopes of catching, if not a whale, at least a minnow. Sometimes she herself is pulled in by a fish too large to handle, but she always reappears with a minnow—sometimes a foolish goldfish—whom, to drop the figure, she marries in haste. Her wildness is always tempered with prudence, and her actions are guided by thoughts of the main chance.

[59] *The Man of Mode,* V, 2.

2. It is possible, of course, that these two characters could have developed in the Restoration, on the foundation of the real but cynical and immoral people of the court, without models in previous drama. But the dramatic precedents are strong, and playwrights capable of developing a new fashion and a new school were not much in evidence during the first decade of the Restoration, when the types first appeared.

These precedents we do not find in the contemporary French comedies, whose plots were so widely borrowed by the English. A comparison of the gallants of Moliere with those of any of the English dramatists who borrowed from him, shows differences so striking as to require little analysis. The French gallant talks, while the Englishman acts; the first deals in wit and universals, playing exhaustively upon ideas, the second deals generally in smut and personalities; the first is proud of his knowledge, his conversational skill, his subtlety, his grace and elegance of deportment; the second—but Lord Stately's remark in Crowne's *The English Friar*, characterizes him:

Ay, there's a folly reigns amongst us; your young fellows now are proud of having no manners, no sense, no learning, no religion, no good nature; and boast of being fops and sots and pox'd in order to be admired.[60]

In English drama antecedent to the Restoration, other than that of Beaumont and Fletcher, we find very little suggestive of this wild couple. There may be, here and there, isolated examples of wild gallants and unconventional ladies in comedy, but I have not been able to find them. They do not appear in the domestic comedy of Heywood and Dekker, Chapman, Middleton and Massinger. In such a comedy as Chapman's *May Day*, we find, in the characters of that most

[60] *The English Friar*, I, 1.

involved intrigue, what are perhaps foreshadowings
of our wild couple. Middleton's Witwoud, in *A Trick
to Catch the Old One*, has some characteristics of the
wild gallant, but he is primarily a guller. In Jonson,
of course, there are no such characters, and in Shakespeare the only close approaches to them are Benedick
and Beatrice, whom the Restoration may have known
through Davenant's *The Law Against Lovers*. In the
Caroline drama we find gallants and ladies who, while
not completely wild and sophisticated, are suggestive
of the Restoration types. And Shirley, Brome, Nabbes,
Cowley and others, all have characters in their comedies who suggest the wild couple without ever being
them. It would be interesting if we could trace the
development of these characters from Beaumont and
Fletcher down through the later Jacobeans and Caro-
lines to the Restoration, but the fact remains that,
whether because the later dramatists were more under
the influence of Jonson, were occupied with other ideas
and problems, or were not sufficiently expert writers,
their conceptions of the wild couple are colorless and
incomplete. Perhaps the Restoration was more fertile
soil. Certainly, to pick a few examples, Brome's Careless, in *The Mad Couple Well Match'd*, is too much of
a prodigal son. Sir Philip and Constance, in *The
Northern Lass*, are nearer the type, but they are over-
shadowed by Jonsonian "humors" characters. Sam
Touchwood and Annabel, in *The Sparagus Garden*, are
gullers and intriguers, but nothing more. Shirley's
characters in *The Changes* are decidedly moral. In his
The Lady of Pleasure, Celestine is a wild young lady,
but her gallant is a stiff, dull nonentity. *Hyde Park*,
often considered a forerunner of Restoration comedy,
has one wild lady in Carol, who, however, is noted

chiefly for railing against marriage; and Fairfield, her consort, is a very colorless character. And we must remember always that the Restoration saw the plays of Beaumont and Fletcher, Shakespeare and Jonson, far oftener than those of any writer contemporary with them in the earlier part of the century.

That the Restoration owed its chief comic personages to Beaumont and Fletcher was recognized somewhat obliquely by Dryden. Discussing the conversation of gentlemen, he says:

That the wit of this age is much more courtly may easily be proved by viewing the characters of gentlemen which were writ in the last. First for Jonson—Truewit, in *The Silent Woman*, was his masterpiece; and Truewit was a scholar-like kind of man, a gentleman with an alloy of pedantry, a man who seems mortified to the world by much reading. The best of his discourse is drawn, not from the knowledge of men, but from books; and, in short, he would be a fine gentleman in a university. Shakespeare showed the best of his skill in his Mercutio; and he said himself that he was forced to kill him in the third act to prevent being killed by him. But, for my part, I cannot find he was so dangerous a person: I see nothing in him but what was so exceedingly harmless, that he might have lived to the end of the play and died in his bed, without offense to any man.

Fletcher's Don John [61] is our only bugbear; and yet I may affirm, without suspicion of flattery, that he now speaks better, and that his character is maintained with much more vigor in the fourth and fifth acts [62] than it was by Fletcher in the three former. [63]

Let us examine this famous Don. In company with his friend, Don Frederick, he is seeking a famous beauty, Constantia. Fate throws Constantia's baby literally into the arms of Don John, and Constantia herself into the arms of Don Frederick. A series of farcical and adventurous episodes follows. Is Don

[61] *The Chances.*
[62] Alteration by George Villiers, Duke of Buckingham.
[63] *Defense of the Epilogue,* Scott-Saintsbury, IV, 239.

John's character that of the typical Restoration gallant? Let us call to witness his landlady, Gillian:

> Oaths! what do you care for oaths, to gain your ends,
> When ye are high and pamper'd? What saint know ye?
> Or what religion, but your purposed lewdness,
> Is to be looked for of ye? Nay, I will tell ye,
> You will then swear like accus'd cut-purses,
> As far off truth, too;[64]

Yet Don John is a gentleman, Dryden assures us. Let us call the gallant as a witness for himself. His friend Frederick has just commended him to Constantia as an honorable man. John is justly angry:

> But you have such a spic'd consideration,
> Such qualms upon your worship's conscience,
> Such chilblains in your blood, that all things pinch you,
> Which nature, and the liberal world, makes custom.
> And nothing but fair honor, oh, sweet honor!
> Hang up your eunuch honor! That I was trusty
> And valiant, were things well put in; but modest!
> A modest gentleman! Oh, wit, where wast thou? [65]

But Dryden might have mentioned others. Here is Monsieur Thomas, from Beaumont and Fletcher's play by that name. His father, Sebastian, fearing (needlessly) that Thomas has decided to reform, resolves to marry again, that he may have a worthy heir. He calls Thomas in. Four of the household maids are present.

SEBASTIAN. For the main cause, Monsieur,
>   I sent to treat with you about, behold it;
>   Behold that piece of story work and view it.
>   I want a right heir to inherit me. . . .
>   And I will break my back but I will get one.

---

[64] *The Chances*, I, 9. (Same in alteration.)
[65] *The Chances*, II, 3. Is it a far cry from John's angry retort to this in Doggett's *The Country Wake*, Act IV, 3?
FLORA.. . . . Where's my cousin?
FRIENDLY. Leave her to my friend's charge—He's an honest gentleman, and will take care of her.
WOODVILLE. A pox of your honest commendations, let me speak for myself, madam, here's your man.

THOMAS. Will you choose there, sir?
SEBASTIAN. There, among those damsels,
    In mine own tribe: I know their qualities,
    Which cannot fail to please me: for their beauties,
    A matter of three farthings makes all perfect,
    A little beer and beef-broth; they are sound too. . . .
    Stand all abreast—Now gentle Master Thomas,
    Before I choose, you having liv'd long with me,
    And happily, sometimes with some of these, too
    (Which fault I never frown'd upon), pray shew me
    (For fear we confound our genealogies)
    Which you have laid aboard; speak your mind freely.
    Have you had copulation with that damsel?
THOMAS. I have.
SEBASTIAN. Stand you aside then.—How with her sir?
THOMAS. How, is not seemly here to say. . . .
SEBASTIAN. Retire you too. Speak forward Master Thomas.
THOMAS. I will and to the purpose; even with all, sir. . . .
SEBASTIAN. What say you to young Luce, my neighbour's
                                      daughter?
    She was too young, I take it, when you travell'd;
                          Some twelve years old.
THOMAS. Her will was fifteen, sir.
SEBASTIAN. A pretty answer! To cut off long discourse,
    For I have many yet to ask you of,
    Where I can choose and nobly, hold up your finger
    When you are right. What say you to Valeria,
    Whose husband lies a-dying now?—Why two,
    And in that form? (i. e. as horns)
THOMAS. Her husband is recovered.[66]

Unquestionably Thomas is a wencher, witty and cynical. He is a scowrer who beats the watch and breaks windows. He is a duellist and a hard drinker. He attempts to seduce his mistress—and he marries her at last, not because he is dying of love, but because the play must come to an end sometime.

Then there is Mirabel, in *The Wild Goose Chase*, who keeps a record book filled with the accounts of

---

[66] *Monsieur Thomas*, IV, 2.

his amorous achievements, who is exceedingly skittish
of marriage, but who succumbs at last to the allure-
ments of a large fortune, later proved to be non-ex-
istent. There are young Loveless and Wellbred, in
The Scornful Lady, two debauched young gentlemen,
and there is the elder Loveless in the same play, a gentleman of the more sober type, one who is concerned
only with getting married. Leandro, in *The Spanish
Curate,* Valentine and Francisco, in *Wit Without
Money,* Jack Wildbrain, in *The Nightwalker,* Claudio,
in *Women Pleased,* Rutillio, in *The Custom of the Country,* Dinant and Cleremont, in *The Little French
Lawyer,* Tibalt, in *The Sea Voyage,* and Cunningham,
in *Wit at Several Weapons*—all are wild gallants,
whose lineal descendants bear their characteristics
through the pages of Restoration comedy. But it is
clear, if we compare these gallants with the later
Restoration types, that the gentlemen of Congreve,
Shadwell, Vanbrugh and Crowne, and their contemporaries, are more wild, more sophisticated, more
artificialized. On the other hand the earlier gallants
of Dryden, Howard and Etherege are less sophisticated
than the Beaumont and Fletcher heroes. The Restoration received the wild gallant and his mistress
from Beaumont and Fletcher but it elaborated and
artificialized them greatly. They became in time, not
so much characters, as symbols for the stock attitudes
toward life in the later decades of the seventeenth century.

The unconventional ladies in Beaumont and Fletcher's dramas, those who, while emancipated in mind and
speech, are moral in action, are well represented by
Margarita, heroine of *Rule a Wife and Have a Wife.*
Desirous of marriage in order that she may enjoy a
plurality of lovers, she is thwarted in her aims by Leon,

her husband, who succeeds in reforming her.   There
is also Dorothea, sister to Monsieur Thomas; and there
is Mary, Thomas' gay and sprightly mistress.   The
otherwise unnamed Scornful Lady belongs to this
group; Rosalura and Lillia Bianca, in *The Wild Goose
Chase,* two merry madcaps seeking husbands, and
Oriana, in the same play, all belong to this group of
husband-seeking, witty, unconventional heroines.

The cynical, thoroughly immoral type of lady is quite
common.   Lillia, in *The Captain,* is so eager for the
delights of love that she makes proposals to her own
father, whom she does not recognize.[67]   Such a situation, we would expect, could end only in tragedy, but
the father merely scolds her, refuses her, and finds her
a husband!   Maria, in *The Coxcomb,* lies with her
husband's best friend, to teach him (the husband) a
lesson![68]   Hippolita, in *The Custom of the Country,*
Annabel, in *The Little French Lawyer,* Amaranta, in
The Spanish Curate, are all women who allow their
desires to dictate their morals.

The better women in the Beaumont and Fletcher
comedies, like those in the Restoration, are virginal
in body, yet at the best they are sufficiently cynical
and knowing to cope with the men on equal terms.
Here, for example, is a peculiar situation from *The
Maid in the Mill.*   Otranto has abducted Florimel, a
lady of the more virtuous type, and endeavored to seduce her.   When he plans to use force she changes her
tactics suddenly from stubborn resistance to extreme
lasciviousness, succeeding in disgusting him:

OTRANTO.   Are you no maid?
FLORIMEL.   Alas, my lord, no, certain!
      I am sorry you are so innocent to think so.
      Is this an age for silly maids to thrive in?

[67] *The Captain,* IV, 3.
[68] *The Coxcomb,* V, 1.

It is so long since I lost it sir,
That I have no belief I ever was one;
What should you do with maidenheads? you hate 'em:
They are peevish, pettish things, that hold no game up,
No pleasure neither; they are sport for surgeons;
I'll warrant you, I'll fit you beyond maidenhead;
A fair and easy way men travel right in,
And with delight, discourse, and twenty pleasures,
They enjoy their journey; madmen creep through
hedges [69]

For a sweet innocent virgin, Florimel is a remarkably good actress.

Such "better" women, with Beaumont and Fletcher, as with the Restoration, are contrasted with women of a much lower moral order. This intensification by contrast may have been further influenced to some extent in the Restoration, by the Beaumont and Fletcher romantic tragi-comedies, in which the contrasts are most striking. Certainly it is an important and effective dramatic device, which can have come only from this one source.[70]

The confidential maidservant, both of the Restoration and the Beaumont and Fletcher drama, must be considered in relation to the wild lady, for she occupies a dual role, that of servant and sometimes bawd, [71]

[69] *The Maid in the Mill*, V, 2.

[70] Thorndike, A. H., *The Influence of Beaumont and Fletcher on Shakespeare*, p. 120. "Each play has one very evil woman and at least one very good one. The evil women, it must be confessed, have more individuality than any other of the characters. . . . In the same way, among the men we find a tendency to intensification and vivid contrast at the expense of all semblance of reality."

The same statements could be applied with almost no change to Restoration comedy.

[71] See for example, this passage from Payne's *The Morning Ramble*, Act I, ii.

HONOUR. Rose, you are a little too wanton.

ROSE (the maid). Madam, you are a little too precise; why, 'tis the bus'ness of a chamber maid to give hints of delight to her lady when they are alone, and there is not one in ten, let them say what they will, but are pleas'd to hear something to the purpose sometimes.

and that of confidant, often playing a part only slightly less important than that of her mistress. She is always an "impudent tom-rig," who is interested in only two things: money and sex. Lionell, the maid in Crowne's *The Married Beau*, well expresses the philosophy of her kind when she says:

In troth, madam, I am stung with a wanton tarantula and shall never be cured till I hear my wedding fiddle; and have danced a jig with my husband in bed. A husband, good Lord, say I.[72]

But the maids did not always require the sanction of the church for their amorous indulgences; frequently they are decidedly wanton. Sometimes they are characterized in the dramatis personae as "a lustful wench," or "a witty maid," the possession of wit seeming to imply a lack of virtue. Any number of such maids may be cited from Restoration comedy. We have Olinda, in Mrs. Behn's *The Dutch Lover*, Mademoiselle, in Vanbrugh's *The Provoked Wife* Prue, in Wycherley's *The Gentleman Dancing Master*, Pindress, in Farquhar's *Love and a Bottle* Bridget, in Shadwell's *The Humorist*, and dozens more. They are all of real importance to the plot, not infrequently managing to capture as husbands a secondary wild gallant.

Here again is a character to be found only in the comedies of Beaumont and Fletcher and those of the Restoration. Bawds and whores are common enough in the older drama; witty maids are not unknown — Maria, in *Twelfth Night* is a good example,—but the waiting maids in general are merely lay figures, subjects for low farce, occasionally, but usually only performers of their allotted duties and no more. Even in the later plays of Brome and Shirley, the immediate

[72] *The Married Beau*, II, 1.

predecessors of the Restoration, the waiting maid is an exceedingly minor character.

The witty, impudent, lustful maid in Beaumont and Fletcher comedies may be well represented by a few examples: Maria, in *The Noble Gentleman*, Juletta, in *The Pilgrim*, Abigail, in *The Scornful Lady*, Panura, in *The Island Princess*, Leucippe, in *The Mad Lover*, and the Nurse and Charlotte, in *The Little French Lawyer*. One or two passages may be quoted to show the characteristics of this type. In *The Little French Lawyer*, when the party with which the nurse is traveling has been captured by supposed bandits, she speaks thus:

> Nay, gentlemen, kind gentlemen,
> Or honest keepers of these woods, but hear me;
> Be not so rough! If you are taken with
> My beauty as it hath been worth the seeking,
> Some one or two of you try me in private;
> You shall not find me squeamish.[73]

Or this, from *The Island Princess*. The Portugese are besieging the castle, and Panura has promised to lead the rebel captain, Piniero, inside the walls by a secret passage:

PANURA. But you must not betray me. You'll offer me no foul
>   play?

> The vault is dark.
PINIERO. 'Twas well remembered.
PANURA. And you may—
> But I hold you honest.
PINIERO. Honest enough, I warrant thee.
PANURA. I am but a poor weak wench! and what with the
>   place,
> And your persuasions, sir—but I hope you will not—
> You know we are often cozened.
PINIERO. If thou dost fear me
> Why dost thou put me in mind?

[73] *The Little French Lawyer*, IV, 6.

PANURA. To let you know, sir,
Though it be in your power and things fitting to it,
Yet a true gentleman—
PINIERO. I know what he'll do:
Come and remember me and I'll answer thee,
I'll answer thee to the full; we'll call at the castle
And then, my good guide, do thy will! Shalt find me
A very tractable man.
PANURA. I hope I shall, sir.[74]

Could Wycherley have had this situation in mind when he wrote *The Gentleman Dancing Master?* Prue, however, has less success than Panura, perhaps because she is dealing with a fool. She tells Monsieur of her dream of being raped by him and ends up with:

Indeed it was so lively, I know not whether 'twas a dream or no. But if you were not there, I'll undertake you may come when you will, and do anything to me you will, I sleep so fast.[75]

But Monsieur is hard to convince. When at last she says she is fearful she may walk in her sleep and so come to his room, he promises to keep his door locked!

4. The other stock figures of Restoration comedy: the eager old lady, the doting heavy father, the jealous and cuckolded husband, and the minor farce figures, are of such wide spread and hazy antecedents that it is difficult to place them in relation to the older drama. Some must have been new inventions; Lady Wishfort, in Etherege's *She Would If She Could,* is certainly the first of the vain, hypocritical, wanton, middle-aged matrons who became stock figures in comedy. The other characters, although they appear in the Beaumont and Fletcher comedies, appear elsewhere in pre-Restoration drama. We can be sure of only three characters taken by the Restoration from Beaumont and Fletcher: the wild gallant, his witty mistress, and the wanton maid servant. These, however, are the

[74] *The Island Princess,* V, 4.
[75] *The Gentleman Dancing Master,* IV, 1.

truly important and distinctive characters of the late seventeenth century comedy. About them the plays are built; their sayings and actions are the main ingredients of Restoration comedy.

Settings

A brief comparison of the settings used in the two groups of comedies may show further likenesses between the old and the new.

The majority of the comedies of the Restoration are set in London, a few in one or other of the various watering places. They are full of the local color of streets, inns, theatres, and parks. Always there is a background of reference to contemporary people and places, people, however, who are always imaginary creations of the author, and places which are more indicated than described. The settings are not realistic in the sense that Jonson's comedies conceive of realism. There is rarely a direct relationship between characters and physical environment. Such a play as *Bartholomew Fair*, with its vivid pictures of places and people, could not have been written in the Restoration.

Of all of Beaumont and Fletcher's comedies only four are set in London,[76] and the London of the Jacobean dramatists is a vague, colorless place, lacking in local color and realistic description. Although the characters are usually given English proper names or punning names, there is very little in their dialogue to indicate that the play might not as well be set in Paris. On the other hand, a play set in a foreign country, Spain or Italy or France, might as well, but for the names, be set in England. The dramatists do not seem to have been interested in local color or consistency.

[76] *Monsieur Thomas*, *Wit at Several Weapons*, *Wit Without Money*, and *The Scornful Lady*.

Such names as Sebastian, Hylas, Valentine, appear in
Monsieur Thomas, supposedly set in London.   Primarily Beaumont and Fletcher were romancers; they
abjured reality of setting.   Again, other of their comedies are given sylvan locations, or bring in a rustic
scene or two. The Restoration conventionalized hatred
for the country is well known.

As far as the realistic London setting is concerned,
there can be only one point of resemblance between
the two groups of comedies, and that is negative.
Neither made use of the true realism as examplified
by Ben Jonson.   There is always an artificial air to
Restoration comedy, as there is to that of Beaumont
and Fletcher.

On the other hand, the Restoration took a vast deal
of interest in Spanish plots,[77] and we find a goodly
number of comedies, — Mrs. Behn's in particular —
which, while making use of English methods, are set
in some artificially romantic Spanish scene. The probability is that Beaumont and Fletcher contributed
largely to the awakening of this interest in things
Spanish, with the notable success of their plays, in
which the Spanish[78] story and setting were important.
Certainly they were not the first to make use of Spanish plots and settings, yet a study of the old plays
which were popular with the Restoration discloses the
fact that other such Spanish influenced comedies are
very rare.

[77] Cf. Nicoll, *Restoration Drama,* p. 180.
[78] Notably *Rule a Wife and Have a Wife, The Spanish Curate, Love's Pil-
grimage, The Chances, The Custom of the Country.*
For contemporary evidence on this point I quote from Cavandish's *The
Triumphant Widow,* Act III. Crambo is ill, and is being fed poetry as a
cure.
CODSHEAD. Good sir, try some English poets, a Shakespeare.
DOCTOR. You had as good give him preserved apricocks, he has too much wit
        for him, and then Fletcher and Beaumont have so much of the
        Spanish perfume of Romance and Novels.

Summary

When the two theatres were opened in 1660 there were practically no new dramas to be had. As a result Killigrew and Davenant turned to the old stock plays, popular before the Restoration. It was years before enough new plays were produced to make a real impression on the stage, and the old plays remained so popular that many of them were revived time after time for decades. Of all these revived plays those of Beaumont and Fletcher, Shakespeare and Jonson were the most popular; the tragi-comedies and comedies of Beaumont and Fletcher exceeding in number and in number of revivals those of the other two dramatists. Their place on the Restoration stage was highly important. Critics, comparing the new age with the old, that is, before the Commonwealth period, had words of praise for no one but Beaumont and Fletcher, Shakespeare and Jonson, speaking of the "learned" Jonson, the "natural" Shakespeare, and the "witty and ingenious" Beaumont and Fletcher. But with learning and nature the Restoration audiences, *not* the critics, had nothing to do; they prized especially those qualities for which Beaumont and Fletcher were praised.

If the Restoration was influenced at all by the drama which preceded the Commonwealth, it must have been influenced by the work of the three great writers (considering Beaumont and Fletcher as a unit) for it rarely mentioned the immediate predecessors of the Commonwealth, and rarely saw their plays. But it could hardly have been influenced in comedy by Ben Jonson. The plays of the great classicist are learned and moral; the Restoration disliked both learning and morality. They are realistic; Restoration comedy is artificial. Their satire is directed against abuses and universal characteristics; that of the Restoration is directed against personalities. And the subject matter of the Restoration, sex and adventure, is far from the subject matter of Jonson. Even the avowed imitators of Jonson did not adhere to their vows. One dramatic method only, the Restoration received in modified form from Jonson, and from Jonson's contemporaries—the "humors" method of characterization, used chiefly in farce.

The Restoration could not have been influenced in comedy by the comedies of Shakespeare; for it rarely saw them. Shakespeare was prized for his tragedies, which were enormously popular; his comedies were neglected.

The Restoration liked the plays of Beaumont and Fletcher, but it altered a number of them, a few comedies, the rest tragedies and tragi-comedies. It rarely altered a comedy which was already popular on the stage; usually it revived in slightly changed form some comedy which had not been presented for years. The alterations represented, not the belief of dramatists and audiences that the play was outmoded, but the need of unscrupulous playwrights to claim as their own the work of other men.

The attitude of the Restoration toward Beaumont and Fletcher is partly indicated by the fact that the later dramatists borrowed scenes, situations and occasional characters from the older plays, and sometimes imitated situations of striking dramatic value. The two Jacobeans were not worshipped as classics; they were made use of as excellent models for would-be successful playwrights.

The two groups of dramas have many traits in common. Both expressed a cynical attitude toward marriage and sex; both dealt in veiled or outright obscenity and in personal, pointed wit. And these characteristics, taken together, make up the Restoration drama. There is nothing more to be found in them. Both groups of dramas made use of certain stock situations of intrigue and adventure; they handled these situations in nearly identical fashions. Both made use of stock characters, and evidence is clear that the chief characters of the later comedy, the wild gallant and his witty mistress, can have come only from the Beaumont and Fletcher comedy. Artificial characters, in artificial settings, going through a series of amorous intrigues, giving utterance to cynical, gay, often suggestive dialogues—this is Restoration comedy and it is also the comedy of Beaumont and Fletcher.

It is impossible to prove that any one dramatist of the Restoration was directly influenced by Beaumont and Fletcher—or by any one else. Undoubtedly many influences were at work in the Restoration, French, Spanish, Italian—the *Commedia del'arte*—English, and the change in manners incident upon the restoration of Charles to his father's throne. But the trend of the English drama shows a clear cut force moving beneath all merely surface mannerisms and styles— the force of English character, which can never become French or Spanish or anything but English, fond of an off-color joke, a lively plot, a set of characters who reflect in some way the contemporary life, even if it be only the life of a small sophisticated coterie. And of all the dramatists whose work appeared before the Restoration, Beaumont and Fletcher most appealed to court and courtier; their dramas continued their popularity in the new period; their dominance over the comedy of the Restoration, although it cannot be measured and bounded, must have been great indeed.

APPENDIX

THE DATA contained in the following lists has been gathered chiefly from Genest's valuable history of the stage, which is known to all students of the drama. Occasional dates for revivals have been gleaned from the records of Sir Henry Herbert, in Professor Adam's edition, and from the documents published by Mr. Nicoll in Appendix B, to his history of Restoration drama. Performances recorded by Pepys, Genest noticed, but more such data has come to light in Wheatley's edition of the diarist, conveniently collated by Miss Macafee in her *Pepys on the Restoration Stage.*

Several additional dates for revivals of Beaumont and Fletcher dramas have been discovered by Professor Sprague and recorded in his *Beaumont and Fletcher on the Restoration Stage.* However, since I wished to keep my records chiefly for comparison of the popularity of the three groups of plays, those of Shakespeare, of Jonson, and of Beaumont and Fletcher, I have not listed these new findings. In all probability the same records used by Professor Sprague would have yielded dates of revivals for plays by Shakespeare and Johnson, but these records are not accessible for me.

LIST I

(Plays belonging to the companies)

A. Plays allotted to Davenant, December 12, 1660.

1. Shakespeare
   The Tempest
   Measure for Measure
   Much Ado About Nothing
   Romeo and Juliet
   Twelfth Night
   Henry VIII
   King Lear
   Macbeth
   Hamlet

2.   *The Duchess of Malfi-Webster*
   The Sophy

3. Right for two months in:
   a. Beaumont and Fletcher
   The Mad Lover
   The Maid in the Mill
   The Spanish Curate
   The Loyal Subject
   Rule a Wife and Have a Wife
   b. Shakespeare
   Pericles

B. Plays allotted to Davenant, August 20, 1668.

1. Shakespeare
   Timon of Athens
   Troilus and Cressida
   Henry VI

2. Beaumont and Fletcher
   Cupid's Revenge
   Women Pleased
   Wit at Several Weapons
   The Woman Hater
   The Faithful Shepherdess
   The Honest Man's Fortune

3. Jonson
   Poetaster

4. By others:

Chapman
All Fools
Biron's Conspiracy
Chabot, Admiral of France
Revenge of Bussy D'Ambois
Revenge for Honor

Day
Humor Out of Breath

Ford
The Broken Heart
Lovers' Melancholy

Habington
The Queen of Arragon

Markham
Hero and Antipater

Mason
Muliasses, the Turk

Randolph
The Jealous Lovers

Shirley
The Bird in a Cage

C. Plays allotted to Killigrew, January 12, 1669 (presumably a re-issue of a document of 1660).

1. Shakespeare
The Winter's Tale
King John
Richard II
Two Gentlemen of Verona
The Merry Wives of Windsor
The Comedy of Errors
Love's Labour's Lost
Midsummer Night's Dream
As You Like It
Taming of the Shrew
All's Well That Ends Well
Henry IV
Richard III
Coriolanus

    Titus Andronicus
    Julius Caesar
    Othello
    Antony and Cleopatra
    Cymbeline

2. *Jonson*
    Everyman in His Humor
    Everyman Out of His Humor
    Cynthia's Revels
    Sejanus
    Volpone
    The Silent Woman
    The Alchemist
    Cataline His Conspiracy
    Bartholomew Fair
    The Staple of the News
    The Magnetic Lady
    The Devil is an Ass
    A Tale of a Tub

3. Beaumont and Fletcher
    The Beggars' Bush
    Bonduca
    The Captain
    The Coxcomb
    The Custom of the Country
    The Double Marriage
    The Elder Brother
    The Faithful Shepherdess
    The False One
    The Fair Maid of the Inn
    The Humorous Lieutenant
    The Island Princess
    A King and No King
    The Knight of Malta
    The Little French Lawyer
    The Laws of Candy
    Love's Cure
    The Lovers' Progress
    The Loyal Subject
    Love's Pilgrimage
    The Maid's Tragedy

The Nice Valour
The Noble Gentleman
Philaster
The Pilgrim
The Prophetess
The Queen of Corinth
Rollo, Duke of Normandy
The Scornful Lady
The Sea Voyage
The Spanish Curate
Thierry and Theodoret
Rule a Wife and Have a Wife
Valentinian
A Wife for a Month
The Wild Goose Chase
The Woman's Prize

4. By others

Carlell
Arviragus and Philicia
The Deserving Favorite
Osmond the Great Turk

Brome
The Northern Lass
The Novella

Chapman
Bussy D'Ambois
The Widow's Tears

Cartwright
The Royal Slave

Berkley
The Lost Lady

Cavendish
The Country Captain
The Variety

Greene
Alphonsos

Howard
The Duke of Lerma

Massinger
  The Duke of Milan
  The Guardian
  The Bashful Lover
  The Emperor of the East
  The Fatal Dowry
  The Roman Actor
  The Unnatural Combat

Middleton
  More Dissemblers Than Women
  The Mayor of Quinsboro
  The Widow

Shirley
  The Doubtful Heir
  The Imposter
  The Brothers
  The Sisters
  The Cardinal

Suckling
  Aglaura
  Brennoralt
  The Goblins

Anonymous
  The Merry Devil of Edmonton
  The Spartan Ladies

LIST II

(Plays by minor pre-Restoration dramatists which appeared during the Restoration)

Berkley
  The Lost Lady
    1661

Brome
  The Antipodes
    1661
    1662

The Jovial Crew
  1661-4
  1669
  1689
  1702-2
  1704-2
  1705
  1707
  1708-4
  1710
  1711
  1712
  1714
  1715
  1716
  1717
  1718
  1719
  1720
Mad Couple Well Matched
  1677—as *The Debauchee; or the Credulous Cuckold—Behn*
The Northern Lass
  1667
  1684
  1710
  1711-2
  1713-2
  1716-2
  1717-2
  1718
  1719
  1720
The Sparagus Garden
  1662

Cavendish
  The Country Captain
    1661

Chapman
  Bussy D'Ambois
    1691—or *The Husband's Revenge—D'Urfey*
  Eastward Ho
    1685—as *Cuckold's Haven-Tate*

Cooke
 Greene's Tu Quoque
  1662 to 1665
  1667
Davenant
 The Unfortunate Lovers
  1660
Field
 A Woman's a Weathercock
  1667
Ford
 The Ladies' Trial
  1669
 'Tis Pity She's a Whore
  1661
Glapthorne
 Argalus and Parthenia
  1661
 Wit in a Constable
  1662
Habington
 The Queen of Arragon
  1668
Heywood, Thomas
 If You Know Not Me, You Know Nobody
  1667
 Love's Mistress
  1661-3
  1665
  1668
Killigrew
 Claricilla
  1660
  1661
Kyd, Thomas
 The Spanish Tragedy
  1668
Marlowe
 Dr. Faustus
  1662
  1686—*as a three act farce—Mountfort*

Lust's Dominion
  1677—as *Abdelazar, or the Moore's Revenge*—Behn
Marston
  The Dutch Curtezan
    1680—*The Revenge, or a Match in Newgate*—Betterton
Massinger
  The Bondman
    1661-4
    1662
    1664
    1666
    1719
  The Fatal Dowry
    1703—as *The Fair Penitent*—Rowe
  New Way to Pay Old Debts
    1677—or *The Credulous Cuckold* (?)
    1708
  Renegado
    1662
  The Virgin Martyr
    1668-3
Mayne
  The City Match
    1668
Middleton
  The Changeling
    1661
  No Wit, No Help Like a Woman's
    1677—*Counterfeit Bridegroom* (?)
  The Spanish Gypsy
    1668
  A Trick to Catch the Old One
    1662 to 1665
  The Widow
    1660
    1661
Randolph
  The Jealous Lovers
    1682
Rowley
  All's Lost by Lust

1661
1705—*as The Conquest of Spain—Pix*
Shirley
  The Brothers
    1662
  The Cardinal
    1662
    1667
    1668
  The Changes
    1662
    1663
    1667
    1668-2
  The Court Secret
    1664
  The Gamester
    1711—*as The Wife's Relief—Johnson*
  The Grateful Servant
    1667
    1669
  Hyde Park
    1668
  Love's Cruelty
    1660
    1667
    1668
  The Opportunity
    1660
  The School of Compliment
    1667
    1668
  The Traitor
    1660
    1661
    1665
    1667
  The Wedding
    1661
  The Witty Fair One
    1667

Suckling
  Aglaura
    1661
    1662
    1668
  Brennoralt
    1661
    1662
    1667
    1668
  The Goblins
    1667-3
Tomkins
  Albumazar
    1668
Webster
  A Cure for a Cuckold
    1696—as *The City Bride—Harris*
  Appius and Virginia
    1670—as *The Unjust Judge—Betterton*
  The Duchess of Malfi
    1662
    1668
    1705—*Unhappy Choice* (?)
    1707—*Unnatural Brothers* (?)
  The White Devil
    1661
Anonymous
  The Merry Devil of Edmonton
    1662
    1691
  Love's Mystery
    1660
  The Dancing Master
    1661
  The French Dancing Master
    1662
  The Contented Colonel
    1662
  Love at First Sight
    1662

LIST III

Revivals of plays by Shakespeare [1]

All's Well That End's Well
Anthony and Cleopatra
   1678—*All for Love; or The World Well Lost—Dryden* [2]
   1718
   1719
As You Like It
The Comedy of Errors
Coriolanus
   1682—*The Ingratitude of a Commonwealth—Tate*
   1718
Cymbeline
1682—*As, The Injured Princess, or The Fatal Wager—*
      D'Urfey
   1702
   1717
   1720-3
Hamlet
   1661-3   Quartos 1603-4-5-11-37
   1662   76-83-95-1703
   1663
   1668
   1673
   1685
   1703
   1705-2
   1706-2
   1707-4
   1708-3
   1709-4
   1710-5
   1711-3
   1712-2
   1713
   1715-3
   1716-5

[1] In Lists III, IV and V, all plays by the respective writers have been listed, revived or not, to show the likes and dislikes of the Restoration audiences.

[2] Where revivals follow an alteration it is impossible to know whether the revival is that of the original or of the alteration.

1717
1718-3
1719-4
1720-3
Henry IV, Part I
1660-2
1661
1667
1668-2
1700
1704-2
1705
1706
1707
1708-2
1710-2
1711-2
1712
1713
1714
1715-3
1716-4
1717
1718-3
1719-2
1720

Quartos 1598-99-1604-8-
13-22-32-39-1700

Henry IV, Part II
1720—*alteration by Betterton*
Henry V
1666
Henry VI, Parts I and II
1681—*alteration by Crowne*
Henry VI, Part III
Henry VIII
1663
1664
1668
1672
1705
1707
1708
1709
1716

1717
1719-2
Julius Caesar

Quartos 1684-91

1676
1684
1687
1704
1706
1707-2
1709
1710
1712
1713-3
1714
1715
1716-3
1718-3
1719
1720
King John
King Lear
1662

Quartos 1608-55

1681—*alteration by Tate*
1687
1702
1703
1705
1706-2
1708-2
1709
1710-2
1711
1712
1713
1714
1715
1716
1717
1718-2
1719
1720-2

Love's Labour's Lost
Macbeth
 1664
 1666
 1667-4
 1668-2
 1669
 1672—*alteration by Davenant*
 1686
 1702
 1703-2
 1704
 1707-3
 1708-4
 1709-2
 1710-3
 1711
 1712
 1713-2
 1714
 1716-2
 1717-3
 1718-3
 1719-2
 1720-3

Measure for Measure   **Quarto 1673**
 1662—*as Law Against Lovers—Davenant (with Much Ado*
  About Nothing)
 1700—*alteration by Gildon*
 1706
 1720

The Merchant of Venice
 1701—*as The Jew of Venice—Granville*
          Quartos—1600-19-37-52
 1706
 1711
 1715
 1717
 1719
 1720

The Merry Wives of Windsor   **Quartos—1602-19-30**
 1660-2

1661
1667
1675
1702—*as The Comical Gallant—Dennis*
1704 (Title restored—perhaps original produced)
1705
1720
Midsummer Night's Dream
  1662
  1668
  1692—altered to an opera
Much Ado About Nothing (see *Measure For Measure*)
Othello
  1660-2   Quartos 1622-30-55-81
  1666   87-95-1705
  1669
  1673
  1675
  1685
  1686
  1704
  1705-3
  1707
  1708
  1709-2
  1710-2
  1711-2
  1712-2
  1713
  1714
  1715
  1716-3
  1717
  1718-2
  1719
  1720-4
Pericles
  1660
Richard II
  1681—*as The Sicilian Usurper—Tate*
  1719—alteration by Theobald

Richard III
    1700—alteration by Cibber
    1704
    1713
    1714-2
    1715
    1717-2
    1719-2
    1720
Romeo and Juliet
    1662 (soon afterward given a happy ending by Howard)
    1680—as *The History and Fall of Caius Marius—Otway*
    1707
The Taming of the Shrew
    1667-2—as *Sauny the Scot—Lacy*
    1692
    1698
    1704-2
    1707-2
    1708
    1711
    1712-2
    1714
    1717
The Tempest
    1667—3—alteration by Davenant and Dryden
    1668-4
    1669
    1672—operatic form
    1677
    1702
    1704
    1705
    1707-3
    1708
    1710
    1712
    1713
    1714
    1715-3
    1716
    1717-3

1718
1720-2
Timon of Athens
  1678—as *The Man Hater*—*Shadwell*
  1703-2
  1704
  1705-2
  1706
  1707-4
  1708
  1709
  1711-2
  1714
  1715
  1717-2
  1719
  1720
Titus Andronicus
  1678—or *The Rape of Lavinia*—*Ravenscroft*
  1704-2
Troilus and Cressida
  1679—or *Truth Found Too Late*—*Dryden*
  1709
  1720
Twelfth Night
  1661
  1663
  1669
  1703—as *Love Betrayed*—*Burnaby*
Two Gentlemen of Verona
The Winters' Tale

Folios 1623-32-63-85

List IV

(*Revivals of Plays by Beaumont and Fletcher*)

The Beggars' Bush; or The Royal Merchant—T. C.
  1660-2
  1661-2   Quartos—1661-1717
  1668   Folio—1647—et. seq.
  1674

The Coxcomb—T. C.   Quarto—1718
  1669   Folio—1647
  1682
Cupid's Revenge—T.   Quartos—1615-30-35
  1668   Folio—1679
The Custom of the Country—C.   Folio—1647
  1667-2
  1701—*As Love Makes a Man* (with *The Elder Brother*)
                          by *Cibber*
  1715-4
The Double Marriage—T.   Folio—1647
  1682
  1687
The Elder Brother—C   Quartos—1637-51-61-78
  1660
  1661   Folio—1679
  1701 (See *The Custom of the Country*)
The Fair Maid of the Inn—T. C. Folio—1647
The Faithful Friends—T. C.
The Faithful Shepherdess—T. C. Quartos—1609-29-34-56
  1663   65
  1668-2   Folio—1679
  1669
The False One—T   Folio—1647
The Honest Man's Fortune—T. C. Folio—1647
The Humorous Lieutenant—T. C. Quarto—1697
  1660   Folio—1647
  1661
  1662
  1663 (for twelve performances)
  1666
  1667
  1683
  1684
  1685
  1686
  1687
  1697
  1704-2
  1706
  1709
  1712
  1713-3

1714
1715-2
1716
1717
1718-2
1719

The Island Princess—T. C.   Quartos — 1669-87-99-
1668-2   1701
1669-3   Folio—1647
1674
1675
1687—alteration by Tate
1689—operatic version—Motteux
1702
1703
1706
1714
1715
1717
1718
1719
1720

A King and No King—T. C.   Quartos—1619-25-31-35
1660   39-55-61-76-93
1662   Folio—1679
1669
1675
1683
1685
1686
1705-2
1706
1707

The Knight of the Burning Pestle—C Quartos—1613-35
1662-2   Folio—1679
The Knight of Malta—T. C.   Folio—1647
1686
The Little French Lawyer—C   Folio—1647
1717   (first in twenty years)
1720
The Laws of Candy—T. C.   Folio—1647
Love's Cure—C   Folio—1647

Love's Pilgrimage—T. C.	Quarto—1718
	Folio 1647
The Lover's Progress—T. C.	Folio—1647
The Loyal Subject—T. C.	Quartos—1700-6
1660	Folio—1647
1661	
1705-3—as *The Faithful General*—"M. N."	
The Mad Lover—T. C.	Folio—1647
1660	
1661-2	
1669	
The Maid in the Mill—C.	Folio—1647
1660	
1661-2	
1662	
1682	
1704	
1710-2	
The Maid's Tragedy—T.	Quartos—1619-22-30-38
1660	41-50-61-86-1704
1661	
1662	Folio—1679
1666	
1667-2	
1668-2	
1682—last act altered by Waller	
1687	
1704	
1706	
1707	
1708	
1710-2	
1715	
1716-2	
1717	
1718	
1720	
Monsieur Thomas—T. C.	Quarto—1639
1661-2	Folio—1679
1662	
1678—as *Trick for Trick*—*D'Urfey*	
The Nice Valor—T. C.	Folio—1647

The Night Walker—C.	Quartos—1640-61
1661	Folio—1679
1662-3	
1682	
1705 (not for six years. 1699?)	
The Noble Gentleman—F. C.	Folio—1647
1688—as *The Three Dukes of Dunstable*—D'Urfey	
Philaster—T. C.	Quartos—1620-22-28-34
1660	39-52-60-87
1661	Folio—1679
1662	
1668	
1673	
1674	
1676	
1695—alteration by Settle	
1711	
1714	
1715	
1716	
The Pilgrim—T. C.	Quarto—1700
1670—alteration by Vanbrugh	Folio—1647
1700	
1703	
1704	
1706	
1707-2	
1709-2	
1710	
1711	
1712	
1713	
1714	
1716-2	
1719-2	
1720	
The Prophetess—T. C.	Quartos—1690
1690—opera by Betterton	Folio—1647
1715	
1716	
1717-2	
The Queen of Corinth—T. C.	Folio—1647

Rollo, or The Bloody Brother—T.
 1661
 1667
 1668
 1674
 1675
 1685-2
 1686
 1705
 1708

        Quartos—1639-40-85
        Folio—1679

Rule a Wife and Have a Wife—C
 1660
 1661
 1662-2
 1663
 1666
 1682
 1683
 1685-2
 1697
 1701
 1703
 1704
 1705
 1706
 1707
 1708-2
 1709
 1711-2
 1712
 1713
 1714
 1715
 1717-3
 1718
 1719

        Quartos—1640-96-97

        Folio—1679

The Scornful Lady—C
 1660-2
 1661-3
 1662
 1666-2
 1667

        Quartos—1616-25-30-
        35-39-51-77-91-95
        Folio—1679

```
            1668-2
            1682
            1683
            1702
            1704
            1708
            1709
            1710
            1711-2
            1713-2
            1714
            1715
            1716
            1718
            1719
```

The Sea Voyage—C   Folio—1647
```
            1667-2
            1668-2
            1685—as A Commonwealth of Women—D'Urfey
            1702
            1706
            1708   (D'Urfey)
            1710-2
            1715
            1716
            1717
            1720
```

The Spanish Curate—T. C.   Quarto—1718
```
            1660                       Folio—1647
            1661-2
            1662
            1669
            1687
```

Thierry and Theodoret—T.   Quartos—1621-48
                                       Folio—1679
The Two Noble Kinsmen—T. C.
```
            1664—as The Rivals—by Davenant Folio—1679
            1667
```
Valentinian—T.   Quartos—1685-96
```
            1679                       Folio—1647
            1682
```

1684—alteration by Rochester
1687
1706-2
1710
1711
1715-2

A Wife for a Month—T. C.   Folio—1647
1660
1661
1697—as *The Unhappy Kindness*—Scott

The Wild Goose Chase—C.   Quarto—1652
1660   Folio—1679
1661
1668
1702—as *The Inconstant*—*Farquhar*

Wit at Several Weapons—C.   Quarto—1639
1709—as *The Rival Fools*—by *Cibbe*Folio—1647

Wit Without Money—C.   Quartos—1639-61-1708
1660-2   Folio—1679
1661
1663
1672
1692
1707-3
1709
1711
1712
1715-2
1716
1717

The Woman Hater—C.   Quartos—1607-47-48
                               Folio—1679

Women Pleased—T. C.   Folio—1647
1668

Woman's Prize—C.   Folio—1647
1660
1661-2
1668
1674

                    First Folio—1647
                    Second Folio—1679
                    Collected edition (Tonson) 1711

(Plays of Ben Jonson Revived)

The Alchemist—C.	Quartos—1612
1661-3	Folio—1616
1664	
1669	
1674	
1675	
1702	
1709-2	
1710	
1711-2	
1713	
Bartholomew Fair—C.	Folio—1640
1661-5	
1664	
1667	
1668-2	
1669	
1674	
1702	
1704-2	
1707	
1708	
1710	
1711-2	
1712	
1713-2	
1715	
1716	
1717	
1718	
1720-3	
The Case is Altered—C.	Quarto—1609
Cataline His Conspiracy—T.	Quartos—1611-35
1668-4	Folio—1616
1675	
Cynthia's Revels—C.	Quarto—1601
	Folio—1616
The Devil is an Ass—C.	Folio—1631 supplement

(Revived between 1663 and 1682)

Everyman in His Humor—C.
  1675
Everyman Out of His Humor—C.
  (Revived between 1663 and 1682)
The New Inn—C.

Mortimer—T.
The Magnetic Lady—C.
Poetaster—C.

Sad Shepherd—Past.
Sejanus—T.
  1660
The Silent Woman—C.
  1660-3
  1661-2
  1664
  1666
  1667
  1668
  1703
  1704
  1707-2
  1708
  1709
  1710-3
  1711
  1713-2
  1714
  1715
  1716-2
  1718-2
  1719
  1720
The Staple of the News—C.
A Tale of a Tub—C.
Volpone—C.
  1665
  1667
  1675
  1703-2
  1704

Quarto—1601
Folio—1616
Quarto—1600
Folio—1616
Quarto—1629
Folio—1631 Sup.
Folio—1640
Folio 1640
Quarto—1602
Folio—1616
Folio—1640
Quarto—1605
Folio—1616
 Quartos—1612-20-1709
Folio—1616

Folio—1631 Sup.
Folio—1640
Quarto—1607
Folio—1616

1705-2
1706
1708
1709
1710
1712-2
1713
1715
1716
1717-2
1718
1720-2

First Folio—1616
Folio II—1640 (1631-41)
Complete Folio—1692
Reprint—1716

SELECTED BIBLIOGRAPHY

ADAMS, J. Q. *The Dramatic Records of Sir Henry Herbert, Master of the Revels,* (1623-1673)—1918

BAKER, D. E. *Biographia Dramatica, or a Companion to the Playhouse*—3 vols., 1812

BEAUMONT AND FLETCHER. *Bullen, edit., Variorum edition,* 4 vols., 1904. *Dyce, Alexander, edit.,* 11 vols., 1843

BELJAME, ALEXANDER. *Le Public et les Hommes de Lettres en Angleterre au dix-huitieme Siecle,* (1660-1744)—1897

BLOUNT, SIR THOMAS POPE. *De Re Poetica, or Remarks Upon Poetry*—1694

BOHN, WM. H. *The Development of John Dryden's Literary Criticism, P. M. L. A., XXII,* 1.

BRADLEY, J. F., AND ADAMS, J. Q. *The Jonson Allusion Book* (1597-1700)—1922

BUTLER, SAMUEL. *Remains*—col. 1729

CASTLEAINE, MAURICE. *Ben Jonson*—1907

CHARLANNE, L. *L'Influence Française en Angleterre au dix-septième Siécle*—1906

COLLIER, JEREMY. *A Short View of the Profaneness and Immorality of the English Stage*—1698

DAVIES, THOMAS. *Dramatic Miscellanies,* 2 vols., 1783

DOBREE, BONAMY. *Restoration Comedy*—1924.

DURHAM, W. H. *Critical Essays of the Eighteenth Century,* 1700-1725—1915

FORSYTHE, R. S. *A Study of the Plays of Thomas D'Urfey*—1916

GAYLEY, C. M. *Francis Beaumont—Dramatist*—1914

GENEST, JOHN. *Some Account of the English Stage from the Restoration in 1660 to 1830.* 10 vols.—1832.

HERFORD, C. H. AND SIMPSON, PERCY. *Ben Jonson*—2 vols.—1925

KERR, MINA. *The Influence of Ben Jonson on English Comedy,* 1598-1642—1912

KRUTCH, J. W.   *Comedy and Conscience After the Restoration*—1924

LANGBAINE, GERARD.   *An Account of the English Dramatick Poets*—1691

LOUNSBURY, T. R.   *Shakespeare as a Dramatic Artist*—1902

MILES, D. H.   *The Influence of Moliere on Restoration Comedy*—1910

NETTLETON, G. H.   *English Drama of the Restoration and Eighteenth Century* (1642-1780)—1914

NICOLL, ALLARDYCE.   *An Introduction to Dramatic Theory*—1923.   *A History of Restoration Drama*—1923.   *A History of Eighteenth Century Drama to 1750*-1926

PALMER, JOHN.   *The Comedy of Manners*—1913

RISTINE, F. H.   *English Tragi-comedy*—1910

SPINGARN, J. E.   *Critical Essays of the Seventeenth Century*, 3 vols.—1908

SPRAGUE, A. C.   *Beaumont and Fletcher on the Restoration Stage*—1926

SYMONDS, J. A.   *Ben Jonson*—1898

THORNDYKE, ASHLEY H.   *The Influence of Beaumont and Fletcher on Shakspeare*—1901

TUPPER, J. W.   *The Relation of the Heroic Play to Beaumont and Fletcher*—P. M. L. A., XX

WARD, A. W.   *History of English Dramatic Literature*, 3 vols.—1899

INDEX

INDEX